T0360615

Social Scientists Confronting Global Crises

This book arose out of a "rant" Ed Schein sent to me in 2020 arguing that social scientists need to address global crises. That is, social scientists already develop knowledge that is directly pertinent to global challenges and crises and need to be included in initiatives taken to address them. They must present their knowledge in public forums and their voices need to be heard by others. This book is a step towards such presentation and involvement.

Social scientists understand ways global crises are crucially intertwined with our relationships, groups, organizations, communities, institutions, how they collaborate with each other, how they compete with each other, and the dynamics intermingled with these. These dimensions are inadequately addressed by scientists and insufficiently recognized by other stakeholders. The social scientists whose work is included in this book are associated with management and have foundational training in all the social science disciplines. They are highly respected internationally. Their work highlighted here contributes to deep understandings of social phenomena associated with global crises. It also demonstrates skilled ways of intervening among those dealing with challenges and crises first-hand. Finally, it also shows the ongoing personal development required to address global crises in productive ways.

This book will be of interest to social scientists, researchers, academics, organizational consultants and students in the fields of management, especially those focusing on global challenges and crises. It will also be a useful resource for practitioners and policy makers.

Jean M. Bartunek is the Robert A. and Evelyn J. Ferris Chair and Professor of Management and Organization at Boston College, USA.

"For those who hold the view that social scientists have little to offer in solving the global crises of our times, this book will change your mind. With inspiring examples of transformative–systemic–collaborative projects, Bartunek and her contributors provide profound insights on how social scientists can be compassionate, courageous, reflective, humble, and objective agents of social change while solving the wickedly complex problems in a threatened and fragile world."

Anne S. Tsui, *Co-Founder, Responsible Research in Business and Management and Professor Emerita, Arizona State University, USA*

"While scientific evidence helps us to grasp the complexity of global crises like climate change and pandemics, we have been missing an important voice. None of these challenges can be faced without social coordination. Finally, we have a book that addresses the relational/social nature of the global crises we face. This collection of authors addresses the multi-dimensional social dynamics at the root of these issues and the relational/organizational interventions that could address them."

Frank J. Barrett, *Professor of Management and Organizational Behavior, Naval Postgraduate School, USA*

"There has never been a greater need for social scientists to collaborate across boundaries to help guide action than today. The global problems we face, from pandemics to climate change, demand it. The authors of this book explain both why and how, providing a hopeful vision for scholars and practice."

Jerry Davis, *Gilbert & Ruth Whitaker Professor of Management and Professor of Sociology, Ross School of Business, University of Michigan, USA*

"There is no time to waste. Management scholars and other researchers need to turn their attention and direct efforts to improve understanding and foster courage to address global crises. This book answers this call. Read it to develop insights and to inspire actions that focus on the relationships, processes, dynamics and systems that are core to global crises and challenges."

Jane E. Dutton, *Robert L. Kahn Distinguished University Professor Emerita of Business Administration and Psychology, University of Michigan, USA*

"This book is both welcome and necessary. Social scientists have so much to add to helping us find solutions to our grand societal challenges, and yet we far too often sit on the sidelines, preferring to remain within the confines of our narrow academic communities. But in this book, noted scholars step out of those confines to engage with our world and bring their knowledge and insights to bear on finding solutions. These solutions do not lie in the next technology alone, but more importantly in the ways we think, act, cooperate and interact. They lie in our culture, institutions, values and beliefs. If you care about solutions to the problems we face, this book offers a critical lens and a model for other scholars to follow."

Andrew J. Hoffman, *Holcim Professor of Sustainable Enterprise, University of Michigan, USA, and author of* The Engaged Scholar *(2021)*

"A treasure chest of powerful and practical ideas generated by extraordinarily talented minds in the social sciences, this book aims to strengthen our ability to confront challenges and crises facing the global community."

Andy Boynton, *John and Linda Powers Family Dean, Carroll School of Management, Boston College, USA*

"The more we are dependent on technology to solve problems, the less we attend to the relevant social and behavioral issues. Just a hypothesis, but even if only half true this book is the kind of contribution that can make a positive impact. Thank you Jean Bartunek, for this significant step in the right direction."

W. Warner Burke, *Professor of Psychology and Education, Columbia University, USA*

"This book is not only a call to action, but also a challenge. In the past decade, attention has grown regarding the need for social scientists to inform the handling of global crises. Additionally, leading social scientists have begun to accept their fundamental obligation to be engaged. Unfortunately, scientists are not trained or rewarded for communicating their relevant knowledge in terms that policy makers, the media, and the public see as helpful or actionable. This book is a timely springboard to speed up that crucial engagement – but only if we concerned scientists truly confront those global crises and commit to acting."

Sim B. Sitkin, *Michael W. Krzyzewski University Professor, Professor of Management and Public Policy, Duke University, USA*

"Social scientists have a responsibility to speak to critical issues of the day. In this book, Jean Bartunek has organized a superb group of scholars to demonstrate how their research on complex organizations can help address our global environmental crisis. Bravo! Now let's put their insights to work before it is too late!"

Thomas A. Kochan, *MIT Sloan School of Management, USA*

"The world is besieged by ever more frequent, intense, and systemic crises. Global crises that technological innovation and market forces cannot solve and often contribute to. These crises are on us. They involve the ways we live and work together. And only finding new ways of living and working together we might work through, resolve, and learn from global crises. This volume provides much needed help from social scientists. It gives voice to scholars and practitioners who have spent a lifetime understanding, supporting, developing, what makes social systems thrive or suffer. Their ideas, advice, and practices to foster collaboration in critical circumstances are actionable and inspiring. The book points us toward the work we need to do to get through crises, together."

Gianpiero Petriglieri, *Associate Professor of Organisational Behaviour, INSEAD, France*

Social Scientists Confronting Global Crises

Edited by Jean M. Bartunek

LONDON AND NEW YORK

First published 2022
by Routledge
2 Park Square, Milton Park, Abingdon, Oxon OX14 4RN

and by Routledge
605 Third Avenue, New York, NY 10158

Routledge is an imprint of the Taylor & Francis Group, an informa business

British Library Cataloguing-in-Publication Data
A catalogue record for this book is available from the British Library

Library of Congress Cataloging-in-Publication Data
Names: Bartunek, Jean M., 1944- editor.
Title: Social scientists confronting global crises /
edited by Jean M. Bartunek.
Description: Abingdon, Oxon ; New York, NY : Routledge, 2022. |
Includes bibliographical references and index.
Identifiers: LCCN 2021043117 (print) | LCCN 2021043118 (ebook)
Subjects: LCSH: Social problems. | Crises. | Social scientists. |
Social sciences.
Classification: LCC HN18.3 .S5967 2022 (print) | LCC HN18.3 (ebook) |
DDC 303--dc23
LC record available at https://lccn.loc.gov/2021043117
LC ebook record available at https://lccn.loc.gov/2021043118

ISBN: 978-0-367-62422-4 (hbk)
ISBN: 978-0-367-62425-5 (pbk)
ISBN: 978-1-003-10937-2 (ebk)

DOI: 10.4324/9781003109372

Typeset in Times New Roman
by Deanta Global Publishing Services, Chennai, India

This book is dedicated, with respect, to the memory of all who lost their lives directly or indirectly due to COVID-19

Contents

Contributors

Pratima (Tima) Bansal is Professor of Sustainability and Strategy at the Ivey Business School at Western University and the Executive Director (and Founder) of the Network for Business Sustainability (www.nbs .net), a growing network of over 35,000 followers from management research and practice committed to advancing sustainable business. Tima also founded Innovation North, which is a research-practice collaborative reimagining corporate innovation to align business value with societal values. Tima is a Fellow of the Royal Society of Canada and a Fellow of the Academy of Management. She also holds an honorary doctorate from the University of Hamburg, Germany.

Jean M. Bartunek holds the Robert A., and Evelyn J. Ferris chair and is Professor of Management and Organization at Boston College. She is a past president of the Academy of Management, from which she won the career distinguished service award. She is also a past Dean of the Fellows of the Academy of management, as well as a Fellow of the British Academy of Management and the Center for Evidence-Based Management. She has served as an associate editor of the *Academy of Management Review*, *Academy of Management Learning and Education*, and the *Journal of Applied Behavioral Science*. Her primary interests center around academic–practitioner relationships and organizational change. Her most recent book, with Robert Macintosh, Katy Mason and Nic Beech, is *Delivering Impact in Management Research: When Does It Really Happen* (Routledge, 2021).

Gervase R. Bushe is Professor of Leadership and Organization Development, Beedie School of Business, Simon Fraser University, British Columbia, and an award-winning author of over 100 papers and four books on organizational change, leadership, teams and teamwork. He is internationally known for his research on, and elaboration of, Appreciative Inquiry. His recent book, *Dialogic Organization Development: The Theory and Practice of Transformational Change*, co-edited with Robert Marshak (2015), builds on his groundbreaking research into how organization development methods can produce rapid transformation. His newest book *The Dynamics of Generative Change* (BMI Publishing, 2020) explains and illustrates the Generative Change Model. His leadership development program, Clear Leadership, supports managers who want to lead highly collaborative teams and organizations through the elaboration of a partnership-based theory of organizational design and leadership. Through the Bushe-Marshak Institute for Dialogic OD he edits the BMI Series in Dialogic OD books, and oversees courses and certification in Dialogic OD.

Tomas Chamorro-Premuzic is an international authority in psychological profiling, talent management, leadership development and people analytics. His commercial work focuses on the creation of science-based tools that improve organizations' ability to predict performance, and people's ability to understand themselves. He is currently the Chief Talent Scientist at ManpowerGroup, cofounder of DeeperSignals and Metaprofiling and Professor of Business Psychology at University College London and Columbia University, New York.

Amy C. Edmondson is Novartis Professor of Leadership and Management at Harvard Business School, Boston, Massachusetts, a chair established to support the study of human interactions that lead to the creation of successful enterprises that contribute to the betterment of society. She has been recognized by the biannual Thinkers50 global ranking of management thinkers since 2011, and most recently was ranked #3 in 2019. She studies teaming, psychological safety and organizational learning, and her articles have been published in numerous academic and management outlets. Her most recent book, *The Fearless Organization: Creating Psychological Safety in the Workplace for Learning, Innovation and Growth* (Wiley, 2019), has been translated into 15 languages. Before her academic career, she was Director of Research at Pecos River Learning Centers, where she worked on transformational change in large companies.

Yabome Gilpin-Jackson is an award-winning scholar–practitioner who has directly led change and transformation as a manager, director and executive leader. In addition, she has supported leaders at all levels in the public, private and non-profit sectors to lead through change and center equity as the founder of Supporting Learning and Development

Consulting Inc. She has been named International African Woman of the Year by UK-based Women4Africa and was the first-ever recipient of the U.S.-based Organization Development Network's Emerging Organization Development Practitioner award. She also received the prestigious 2018 Harry Jerome Professional Excellence Award in Canada. She is currently Chair of the Board of Trustees of the Organization Development Network. Yabome holds a PhD in Human & Organization Systems from Fielding Graduate University where she has twice been named an Institute for Social Innovation Scholar/Fellow. She is an Adjunct/Sessional Faculty member at Simon Fraser University, British Columbia, Concordia University, Montreal, Quebec and elsewhere.

Rebecca Henderson is one of 25 University Professors at Harvard University, a research fellow at the National Bureau of Economic Research and a fellow of both the British Academy of Arts and Sciences and of the American Academy of Arts and Sciences. Her research explores the degree to which the private sector can play a major role in building a more sustainable economy. She sits on the boards of Idexx Laboratories and of CERES. Her most recent publication is *Reimagining Capitalism in a World on Fire* (PublicAffairs, 2020), which was shortlisted for the FT/McKinsey 2020 Business Book of the Year Award.

Jody Hoffer Gittell is Professor of Management at Brandeis University's Heller School for Social Policy & Management, Waltham, Massachusetts and cofounder and board member of the Relational Coordination Collaborative. She is interested in how stakeholders achieve their desired outcomes by coordinating with each other. For this purpose, she developed Relational Coordination Theory, which proposes that highly interdependent work is most effectively coordinated through relationships of shared goals, shared knowledge and mutual respect, supported by frequent, timely, accurate, problem-solving communication. The Relational Model of Organizational Change shows how stakeholders can join together to design structural, relational and work process interventions to support more effective coordination of their work. She is currently exploring the relational dynamics of multi-level systems change in complex systems in multiple sectors around the world.

Sandra Janoff, PhD, co-developed the methodology called Future Search, a process used worldwide to get the "whole system" focusing on the future, creating values-based action strategies and securing commitment to implementation She is also co-author of *Future Search: Getting the Whole System in the Room for Vision, Commitment and Action*,

3rd edn (Berrett-Koehler, 2010), along with other books. She works with communities all over the world. As just one example, Sandra's work on humanitarian issues includes UNICEF's Finding a Future for the Children of South Sudan during the North/South Sudanese civil war. This resulted in the demobilization of over 13,000 child soldiers. She is Director of Future Search Network (FSN), a collaboration of members worldwide dedicated to providing Future Search meetings in communities for whatever they can afford. She has won both the Global Work Award and the Lifetime Achievement Award from the Organizational Development Network.

Adam Kahane is a Director of Reos Partners. He is a leading organizer, designer and facilitator of processes through which business, government and civil society leaders can work together to address pressing challenges. He has worked in more than 50 countries, in every part of the world, with executives and politicians, generals and guerrillas, civil servants and trade unionists, community activists and United Nations officials, clergy and artists. Adam is the author of *Solving Tough Problems: An Open Way of Talking, Listening, and Creating New Realities* (Berrett-Koehler, 2007), *Power and Love: A Theory and Practice of Social Change* (Berrett-Koehler, 2010), *Transformative Scenario Planning: Working Together to Change the Future* (Berrett-Koehler, 2012), *Collaborating with the Enemy: How to Work with People You Don't Agree with or Like or Trust* (Berrett-Koehler, 2017), and *Facilitating Breakthrough: How to Remove Obstacles, Bridge Differences, and Move Forward Together* (Berrett-Koehler, 2021).

Chelsea Lei is a doctoral student in management and organization studies at Boston College, Massachusetts. Her research interests center on collaborative practices that connect societal, organizational and personal change, a line of inquiry sparked by her prior experience working in American local government and co-creating a large-scale learning network for public service professionals on performance measurement and continuous improvement. Currently Chelsea is studying the emergence and evolution of a visual collaborative practice known as graphic facilitation.

Colleen Magner is a Director of Reos Partners and leads the Africa team. Colleen's experience includes convening, organizing and facilitating short- and long-term relationships across sectors that address their most pressing challenges – from violence against women to climate change adaptation in vulnerable parts of the African continent. Colleen is also a scenario-planning expert and has led a number of transformative scenario planning processes around the world. She co-authored *Mapping Dialogue: Essential Tools for Social Change*, which outlines a variety of transformative dialogue tools and change processes. She is an adjunct faculty member at the University of Pretoria's Business School, the Gordon Institute of Business Science, South Africa.

Robert J. (Bob) Marshak is Distinguished Scholar in Residence Emeritus in the School of Public Affairs at American University, Washington, DC and has educated thousands of participants in the theories and practices of organizational development at universities and institutes around the world. He has also consulted for more than 40 years with executives in the public and private sectors about organizational change. He is the author of four books and more than 100 articles and book chapters about organizational change. His most recent book is *Dialogic Process Consulting: Generative Meaning-Making in Action* (2020). He is internationally known for his pioneering work on covert processes in organizations, the use of metaphors and symbolic meaning in organizational change and, with Gervase Bushe, the development of Dialogic OD theory and practice. His contributions to the field of organization development have been recognized by numerous awards including the Organization Development Network's Lifetime Achievement Award.

Henry Mintzberg holds the Clegorn Chair of Management Studies in the Desautels Faculty of Management at McGill University. He is a writer and educator, mostly about managing organizations, developing managers, and rebalancing societies, where his attention is currently focused (RebalancingSociety.org). He cofounded and remains active in the International Masters Program for Managers (impm.org) and the International Masters for Health Leadership (mcgill.ca/imhl) as well as a venture called CoachingOurselves.com, all novel initiatives for managers by learning together from their own experience, the last in their own workplace. He has been elected to the Order of Canada and l'Ordre national du Quebec as well as to the Royal Society of Canada. His 20 books have earned him 21 honorary degrees.

Otto Scharmer is a Senior Lecturer in the MIT Sloan School of Management, Cambridge, Massachusetts and cofounder of the Presencing Institute. He introduced the concept of "presencing" – learning from the emerging future. His most recent book, T*he Essentials of Theory U* (2018), summarizes the core principles and applications of awareness-based systems change. In 2015, he cofounded the MITx u.lab and in 2020 the GAIA journey (Global Activation of Intention and Action), both of which activated a vibrant worldwide ecosystem of transformational change. Most recently, his methods and tools have been used to support thousands of change makers in the United Nations to achieve the Sustainable Development Goals. He is a member of the UN Learning Advisory Council for the 2030 Agenda, the World Future Council, and the Club of Rome's High-Level 21st Century Transformational Economics Commission. In 2021 he received the Elevating Humanity Award from the Organizational Development Network.

Edgar H. Schein is the Society of Sloan Fellows Professor of Management Emeritus at the MIT Sloan School of Management, Cambridge, Massachusetts. During his career, he has investigated organizational culture, process consultation, research process, career dynamics and organization learning and change, and made important contributions to each. Besides his numerous articles in professional journals, he has authored 14 books. His books on organizational culture, especially *Organizational Culture and Leadership*, have essentially defined organizational culture for academics and managers. He has received many honors and awards for his writing, including the distinguished Scholar–Practitioner Award of the Academy of Management, 2009, the Lifetime Achievement Award in Workplace Learning and an Honorary Doctorate from the IEDC Bled School of Management in Slovenia. He was educated at the Universities of Chicago, Stanford, and Harvard (PhD 1952).

Peter A. Schein is the cofounder of the Organizational Culture and Leadership Institute (OCLI.org), which is dedicated to advancing organizational development and design through a deeper understanding of organizational culture and leadership theory. His expertise draws on over 30 years of industry experience in marketing and corporate development at technology pioneers including Pacific Bell, Apple, Silicon Graphics, Inc., Packeteer (BlueCoat) and Sun Microsystems, Inc., with a focus on the underlying organizational culture challenges that growth engenders in innovation-driven enterprises. He is co-author of four books with Ed Schein including their most recent release, *Humble Inquiry*, 2nd edn (2021). Peter was educated at Stanford and Northwestern (MBA, 1991).

Peter M. Senge is the founding chair of the Society of Organizational Learning, a global network of organizations, researchers, and consultants dedicated to the "interdependent development of people and their institutions". He is also a Senior Lecturer, Sloan School of Management MIT, Cambridge, Massachusetts and cofounder of the Academy for Systemic Change, which seeks to accelerate the growth of the field of systemic change worldwide. His work centers on promoting a shared understanding of complex issues and shared leadership for healthier human systems. This involves major cross-sector projects focused on global food systems, climate change, regenerative economies and the future of education. He is the author of *The Fifth Discipline* (over two million copies sold) and co-author of several related Fieldbooks. Recently, he was named to the "1000 Talents" Program (Renzai) in China to help China become a leader in systemic change, to benefit itself and the world.

Garima Sharma is an Assistant Professor at the Andrew Young School of Policy Studies, Georgia State University. She holds a PhD from Case Western Reserve University and was a Postdoctoral Fellow at Ivey Business School, Ontario, Canada. Her research focuses on sustainability and the related tension of purpose and profits. She is also interested in understanding how research impacts practice, and the topics of rigor–relevance and knowledge co-creation. Over the years, she has received several grants to support her research.

Shyamal Sharma is a Visiting Research Scholar at Brandeis University's Heller School for Social Policy and Management, Waltham, Massachusetts, funded by The Topol Family Foundation since June 2019. She was the Principal Investigator under a 2000–2002 AHRQ grant for innovative applications of technology for enhancing patient self-management of chronic conditions. During the same years, she worked as the Project Director for a NIH-funded longitudinal study of vulnerable adults with substance use and mental health disorders. She has a diverse background in high-impact issues in health policy, healthcare delivery and public health. She led the 1998 health insurance study that generated crucial policy-relevant information for eventual health insurance reform in Massachusetts. Over a decade later, she returned to the public sector to serve as the quality director of MassHealth Managed Care Programs.

Acknowledgments

I thank all the authors for your contributions. I am also very grateful to Keith Arnold, Nic Beech, Naomi Round Cahalin, Cary Cooper, Terry Clague, Carlota Duarte and other Religious of the Sacred Heart, Linda Ducharme, Kathy Kram, Michael Smith, Christopher Soldt and Alina Gomez Thompson for your assistance, support, skillful editing and helpful comments.

1 Introduction

The importance of this book

Jean M. Bartunek

Executive Summary

This book recognizes social scientists' knowledge and insight pertinent to global crises, and both challenges and enables social science academics and consultants to understand and develop responses to them. In this first chapter, I introduce the book and the impetuses for it. I also indicate some of the range of venues in which social scientists can contribute, including relationships across groups and organizations, political, national and cross-national systems, and development in our capacity for productive action.

Social scientists have knowledge and insights that are directly pertinent to global challenges and crises. We need to be included in initiatives taken to address them. So we need to speak to such issues, to make evident the kinds of contributions we can distinctly offer. This book provides one step towards accomplishing this purpose.

It is not just geologists who understand what is involved in climate change, its causes and its impacts, and not just virologists and epidemiologists who understand pandemics and how to deal with them. Social scientists understand how such crises are intertwined with us as individual human beings, in our relationships, our groups, our organizations, our communities, our institutions, how we collaborate with each other, how we compete with each other, and their ensuing dynamics. Many social scientists, including those featured in this book, have demonstrated great skill in working with these dynamics in practice settings.

Consider the limitations of two recently published influential books. Bill Gates's (2021) *How to avoid a climate disaster: The solutions we have and the breakthroughs we need,* says very little about cooperation and collaboration among groups other than acknowledging various barriers. Yet successful interactions such as those the social scientists included in this book explain and help to create are necessary for people, groups, organizations and nations to carry out the steps Gates recommends for responding to very real climate concerns. Jacqueline Novogratz's (2020) *Manifesto for a moral revolution:*

DOI: 10.4324/9781003109372-1

Practices to build a better world, alludes to the value of trusted relationships, but does not focus on their complexities and what is required for them to be built up and sustained. Yet, developing and sustaining complex relationships are crucial as the contributors to this book show. Thus, this book does not focus so much on specific global crises, but more on the kinds of interactions, relationships and development that affect our ability to deal with them.

The impetus for this book

In April 2020, early in the "lock down" period of the COVID-19 pandemic in the US, Ed Schein, Professor Emeritus at MIT, and a longtime friend, sent me a "call to action" for social scientists and asked me to post it online to stimulate discussion among a group of scholars and consultants concerned about global crises. Ed's call to action forms the appendix of this book. It begins with the admonition that we as social scientists need to *speak up*. It asks the question:

> Will we recognize that we need to use or invent methods of collaboration on a global level to deal with the global environment as a finite resource that we are currently depleting by encouraging or at least sanctioning rampant competition among countries, industries, and political parties?

At the time Ed wrote, I had been rereading my favorite book from my college days, Albert Camus's (1948) novel *The Plague*. In this novel, Camus has Dr. Bernard Rieux, a physician, narrate the story of what happened in Oran, Algeria, when a plague appeared somewhat mysteriously, devastated the town over an extended time period, then ran its course and faded away in a manner also mysterious. Camus describes how several individual citizens of Oran responded to the plague, so the reader gets a chance to see very different personalities interpreting it. Contrary to any effort to separate the "good" people and the "bad" people in a situation like this, one of the things Dr. Rieux learned from the plague was "there is more to admire in men than to despise" (p. 278).

On the very last page of that book, Dr. Rieux described the reason he had decided to narrate the story of the plague. He said that he:

> had resolved to compile this chronicle so that he should not be one of those who hold their peace but should bear witness in favor of those plague-stricken people; so that some memorial of the injustice and outrage done them (by the plague) might endure.

These two sources coming in tandem, Ed's call to action and Camus' book (see Bartunek, in press, for a fuller account), inspired my resolve to compile *this* chronicle. More, I wanted to dedicate the book to those who have passed away due, directly or indirectly, to COVID-19 as one small memorial.

This book is not a narrative about the progression and departure of COVID, which at the time of publication is still devastating many people's lives. Rather, it is a way of enabling sophisticated social scientists who are involved in both academia and practice to show what social scientists can do to address and mitigate (if not prevent) global crises confronting us now and predictably (Bazerman & Watkins, 2004; Phan & Wood, 2020) in the future, and to have empathy for those who suffer from these crises.

The social scientists who have contributed to this book

The contributors to this book are primarily associated with management and organizations, some with a primary emphasis on academic scholarship, some with a primary emphasis on consulting practice, but all with considerable capability and interest in both realms. They all have extensive training in the core social science disciplines that underlie management and organizational studies, including such fields as psychology, sociology, anthropology, economics and political science.

When I invited the authors to contribute, I told them that the only requirement was that each chapter include "something explicit about academic social science scholarship and something that makes the scholarship doable in practice". This book thus represents an academic–practitioner collaboration (Bartunek & McKenzie, 2018), in the sense that both academic and consultant authors are contributing insights on their own terms that together form a whole. Joining the contributions of rigorous scholarship with skilled practice can together lead to a new appreciation of both, contributions that neither could make on their own.

Everyone writing in this book is doing so based on their care for the well-being of our world as well as their skilled and creative thinking and practice; they are all engaged scholars (Hoffman, 2021; Howard-Grenville, 2021; Williams & Whiteman, 2021). The chapters in this book give us hope for our collective future, at least if we are brave enough to respond to the invitations they present us.

Types of contributions in each chapter

The chapters make three types of contributions. They stimulate our *imagination*, showing us creative ways of thinking about positive aspirations for humanity and our relationships even in the midst of global challenges and crises. They motivate us by suggesting some valuable *outcomes* that may be aimed for in response to these challenges and conveying the value of striving for these outcomes. Finally, they discuss particular *actions* that may help accomplish the outcomes. How the chapters accomplish each of these is summarized in Table 1.1.

Table 1.1 What the chapters invite us to *imagine*, what they suggest about possible *outcomes* and types of *actions* they describe

The authors and their chapters	What the chapters help us **imagine**	What the chapters suggest about **outcomes** *for which we can strive*	What the chapters suggest about **actions** *that can help accomplish the intended outcomes*
2. Sandra Janoff Striving for wholeness: It is time for social scientists to make a loud noise!	Differentiation/Integration Theory and Open Systems Theory are the basis for successful whole systems transformation. Bringing together those with authority, resources, expertise, information and those impacted will ensure integrated, sustainable futures.	Global challenges are successfully acted on in creative ways as groups discover more capacity to manage turbulence and complexity.	The Future Search approach enables large diverse groups to create conditions where interdependent stakeholders from within and outside the system can differentiate their perspectives, create a shared future and act together.
3. Pratima (Tima) Bansal and Garima Sharma The important role of management researchers in addressing global crises: Insights from Innovation North	Social scientists often rely on past data to understand and predict the future through models and frameworks. Yet, social scientists can also help shape the future by offering companies not just knowledge, but tools to innovate products and services for a better future for both business and society.	Businesses and social scientists imagine and construct a better society for all.	Social scientists work closely with managers to share knowledge and experiences to co-create tools that navigate the turbulence and unpredictability of global crises.
4. Gervase R. Bushe and Robert J. Marshak Dialogic Organization Development and the Generative Change Model: Opportunities and challenges for managing global crises	Dialogic OD methods and the Generative Change Model are more effective for managing complex, adaptive challenges than planned change approaches.	Dialogic change approaches used successfully in multi-stakeholder situations.	Creating unifying foundations for convivial emergent change and the importance of providing adequate sponsorship to amplify and embed what emerges.

5. Colleen Magner and Adam Kahane When the stakes are high and trust is low	An unconventional, uncomfortable "stretch" approach to collaboration.	Highly diverse teams (even people who do not agree with or like or trust each other) finding ways to move forward together – to achieve collectively what they cannot achieve separately.	Practices for embracing conflict as well as connection, experimenting as a way forward, and recognizing one's own role in the game.
6. Rebecca Henderson Should capitalism be reimagined? If so, how?	Businesses have a compelling economic case for supporting the health of the natural, social and institutional systems in which they are embedded.	Private businesses can solve public problems and help rebuild an inclusive society.	There are multiple illustrations of businesses creating both private profit and public benefit and driving social change through coordinated action.
7. Henry Mintzberg Pathway to balance	Imagine a reformation that takes countries and this globe away from the "isms" and back to balance.	A world where governments of the public sector are respected, businesses of the private sector are responsible and community associations of the plural sector function are robust and thus function in dynamic balance.	Reformation begins on the ground when concerned people ask "What can I do?" and "What can we do, in our communities, businesses, and governments?"
8. Yabome Gilpin-Jackson Gathering on the Bridge: Co-creating our emerging equity-centered future	Polarized privileged and marginalized systems join instead of judging each other from afar.	System wholeness at the gathering place on the bridge.	Systemic changes in the hardware and software of organizations and Edgewalkers doing bridge work between privileged and marginalized systems.

(Continued)

Table 1.1 (Continued)

The authors and their chapters	What the chapters help us **imagine**	What the chapters suggest about outcomes for which we can strive	What the chapters suggest about actions that can help accomplish the intended outcomes
9. Shyamal Sharma and Jody Hoffer Gittell Expanding relational coordination to tackle global crises: The Relational Society Project	Human beings have the capacity for empathy, solidarity, resilience – and the capacity to embrace their interdependence.	Relational society as a state of generalized reciprocity and robust social capital, created through goodwill, empathetic fellowship, and virtuous social interactions.	Interdependent stakeholders engage in coordinated collective action, supported by equitable social and fiscal policies and collaborative structures.
10. Edgar H. Schein and Peter A. Schein Global warming: The threat and the hope	Anticipating a global *meta culture* that prioritizes open and trusting relationships on a global scale.	We may begin to see a global consciousness that integrates both the competitive needs of geopolitical actors with our more human need to collaborate for our survival on this planet.	Our challenge is to foster a new set of more *positive relationships* among us that are less competitive, less nationalistic, more personal and more collaborative.
11. Amy C. Edmondson and Tomas Chamorro-Premuzic Leadership in times of upheaval: The rise of the empathic leader	The stereotypical model of the importance of a commanding leader during crisis is wrong, and needs to be replaced by a model of empathic leadership.	Empathic leadership helps people and organizations to navigate novel, challenging, uncertain contexts.	The importance of empathic leadership, which demonstrates a capacity to connect emotionally with followers, lies in its role in helping them cope with new, challenging, fast-changing situations.

12. Peter M. Senge Renewing the Earth starts with renewing our capacity to work together	We live in a time of a possibility for deep cultural change where, gradually, regenerative development (humans acting as part of nature and guided by nature's capacity to regenerate) could displace today's exploitative model and its destruction of both natural and social capital.	Ideas like circular economies and "net zero" (GHG) energy appeal to many but threaten many others. Building capacity for systemic collaboration can bridge these divides by engaging diverse actors in deeply reflective change processes around aims that have shared meaning.	Systemic collaboration can only arise from ongoing capacity building woven into collaborative work. Developing capacities for seeing systems, fostering aspiration and reflective conversation at scales commensurate with systemic problems demands, paradoxically, starting small with pilot groups where people learn first-hand how to show up differently and then building on existing infrastructures to grow.
13. Otto Scharmer The social field as a teacher: Seven principles for building transformational learning infrastructures	To change a system, you must transform consciousness, and that cannot be done unless you can make a system sense and see itself.	Upgrading the operating system of our global economy from ego-system to eco-system awareness.	The creation of deep learning infrastructures across institutions that help systems and their leaders to sense and see themselves *from the whole* and thus activate the ego to eco shift at all levels of scale.
14. Chelsea Lei Being in service of collaboration: Reflection of a newcomer	Social science is seeking to increase our understandings about what could make it easier for humans to work well together given all that we know about the odds against it.	Emerging from the contributions of this book is a reflective image of interconnected humans who, while boundedly rational, are also capable of being *unboundedly relational*.	It is essential that scholars take time and care to collaborate with and learn from practitioners experienced in facilitating cross-boundary collaborations for solving complex problems.

The grouping of the chapters

I have grouped the chapters into three sets, based loosely on sets of relationships, systems, and types of development to which they invite us to attend. The first set of chapters draws our attention to *relationships across groups and organizations*. Sandra Janoff describes the impact of Future Search Principles on complex issues, showing how the diversity of a system builds capacity for transformational change. Pratima (Tima) Bansal and Garima Sharma describe the creative means they have developed through which managers and academics can jointly develop tools and knowledge to help navigate global crises. Gervase R. Bushe and Robert J. Marshak update their Generative Change Model for societal settings and describe ways that sponsorship and convivial emergence are necessary for successful change in such settings. Colleen Magner and Adam Kahane describe means they have developed across multiple continents that, through stretch collaboration, enable people and groups who do not trust or like each other to work together.

The second set of papers draws our attention to *political, national* and *cross-national systems*. Rebecca Henderson shows that while capitalism has in many cases led to very negative consequences it can contribute positively to institutional systems, and suggests how this may happen. Henry Mintzberg suggests that countries have lost their balance in a set of "isms", and maps out ways they can regain it that will require coordinated efforts from all of us. Yabome Gilpin-Jackson suggests ways that privileged and marginalized systems may gather by means of "bridge work". Shyamal Sharma and Jody Hoffer Gittell describe the efforts of the Relational Society Project to bring together communities in multiple countries to solve population health. Edgar A. Schein and Peter H. Schein conceive of an emerging global metaculture that may overcome competition between nations in order to foster survival on our planet.

The third set of papers draws our attention to *development, and how to foster it*. Amy C. Edmondson and Tomas Chamorro-Premuzic describe how empathic leadership that connects emotionally with followers is necessary for helping followers deal with complex crises. Peter M. Senge discusses the lifetime work of individual and group capacity building in collective reflection and "seeing systems" that is necessary for systemic collaboration. Otto Scharmer discusses learning structures that he and his colleagues are creating that facilitate letting go and activating the capacity for transformational change, among large numbers of people and groups. Finally, Chelsea Lei describes how her practitioner experience of and reflection on the types of work described in these other chapters brought her into a doctoral program that addresses organizational change and helps her recognize the importance of relationality.

I encourage you to read each of the chapters, which make evident how much skilled social scientists can contribute to our world. I invite you to engage with the chapters and their authors, in conversation, in theory and in practice.

References

Bartunek, J. M. (In Press). The fellows and a book: Unexpected opportunities for practice and theory. In L. Browning, J. Sørnes, & P. J. Svenkerud (Eds.), *Organizational communication in the time of coronavirus: Ethnographies and the future of work.* London: Palgrave.

Bartunek, J. M., & McKenzie, J. (Eds.). (2018). *Academic – Practitioner relationships: Developments, complexities, and opportunities.* London: Routledge.

Bazerman, M. H., & Watkins, M. (2004). *Predictable surprises: The disasters you should have seen coming, and how to prevent them.* Boston: Harvard Business Press.

Camus, A. (1948). *The plague,* trans. Stuart Gilbert. New York: Vintage.

Gates, B. (2021). *How to avoid a climate disaster: The solutions we have and the breakthroughs we need.* New York: Knopf.

Hoffman, A. J. (2021). *The engaged scholar: Expanding the impact of academic research in today's world.* Redwood City: Stanford University Press.

Howard-Grenville, J. (2021). Caring, courage and curiosity: Reflections on our roles as scholars in organizing for a sustainable future. *Organization Theory, 2*(1), 1–16.

Novogratz, J. (2020). *Manifesto for a moral revolution: Practices to build a better world.* St. Martin's Griffin.

Phan, P. H., & Wood, G. (2020). Doomsday scenarios (or the black swan excuse for unpreparedness). *Academy of Management Perspectives, 34*(4), 425–433.

Williams, A., & Whiteman, G. (2021). A call for deep engagement for impact: Addressing the planetary emergency. *Strategic Organization, 19*(3), 526–537. doi:10.1177/14761270211011703

Part I

Attention to relationships across groups and organizations

2   Striving for wholeness

It is time for social scientists to make a loud noise!

Sandra Janoff

This is a grave moment in time! We are being pounded by a torrent of crises, each colliding with the other, and impacting everyone on the planet: Global warming, worldwide pandemics, rising fascism, racial injustice, refugee crises, mental health crisis, economic devastation, global and local inequalities. Our fragmented systems are broken and collapsing in front of us. We are drowning in the flood and turning against each other in rage. Differing views have turned into opposition. Frustration and anxiety have turned into fear and aggression. We do not see our shared suffering. We question whether we have what it takes to alter the course. Physicist David Bohm said, "reality is a seamless whole" (1996). Biologist Ludwig von Bertalanffy said, "everything is connected to everything else" (1952). These theoretical scientists have a message that we social scientists cannot ignore. Clearly, we must see the urgency of our work. We must enable people to experience their interconnectedness and develop a combined capacity to navigate these rapids. We must do this before the damage is irreversible. In this chapter I will share my perspective on why systems are broken. I will also share my experience working with intractable issues that cross many boundaries and end with my call to social scientists to leverage our role in achieving a world that works for all.

Brokenness in systems at every level

Why then are most systems breaking down? We are in dreadful uncertainty and lack the economic, environmental or leadership conditions we need to adapt. Many communities are bitterly polarized around politics that strangle their most pressing concerns. Many corporate environments are demoralizing and draining creative energy. Leaders tend to strategize with those closest to them in the hierarchy. Those who are not in the dialogue have no influence in improving things.

DOI: 10.4324/9781003109372-3

Imagine getting diverse people to grapple with controversial economic and social issues. It would mean planning with a full spectrum of perspectives, including those impacted by the outcomes. This is a big step for many leaders who fear they will lose control and chaos will ensue. It takes faith that, at our core, our common humanity matters more than our differences. We are at a point in time when we must take a leap of faith into unknown territory. We no longer have a choice.

Where is our hope?

Counter to the nightmare reality I have just described is another reality that is spectacular. We are slowly moving out of denial! There is a reawakening. Our need for connection has become clearer as the pandemic forced us to stay apart. Acts of oppression, aggression and political extremism in many Western countries are exposing our racism, sexism, homophobia, transphobia, Islamophobia, antisemitism and xenophobia. These *isms* are so real there is no more room for denial of their existence at the heart of our societies. But, they are *not* the heart of us. While it is not uncommon in times of fear and distrust to look for scapegoats, we are beginning to see that we can do better. We are starting to cross boundaries of race, culture, gender, age and economic status to confront social justice, health and climate. The path forward is working *with* our differences and paying attention to *how* we structure the forums in which we take on these intractable problems. Transformation means doing something different – including diverse perspectives and creating conditions for learning, discovery and action. I ask us, as social scientists, if transformation does not take place in our forums, how can we expect it to take place in society?

What does transformation look like?

I remember vividly the first day of a graduate clinical psychology class. The professor said, "Well, since you are studying to be psychologists, you want to help individuals change. I assume you have a theory of change". That semester he taught us *his* theory of change, but that question never left my mind. Social scientists are in the *business of change* and our assumptions about what works are our starting point. In this clinical psych class I learned the difference between behavior change and structure change. I now embrace a structural theory of change. I emphasize this for three reasons. First, the world is moving too fast to assume we can change big systems one individual at a time. Second, I believe the increasing diversity in our communities and workplaces is our asset. Creating structures to leverage that asset is our hope for transformation. Third, we are more distrusting of leaders, systems and each other than ever before. My lens enables distrust to take a back seat to discovering common ground. Trust finds its way forward.

My lens for systems change: Differentiation/Integration Theory (D/I)

D/I theory has a long history in biology, mathematics and developmental psychology, but a short history in organization and community work. It says: Systems develop through ongoing differentiation and integration (Agazarian, 1997). Differentiation means learning more about different perspectives. Integration means taking in the differences as resources. As I will discuss below, I apply this abstract theory by bringing people with diverse views together, providing opportunities to differentiate based on function or experience and supporting dialogue as they build capacity to solve complex problems. That is *real* integration. But – there's an irony that makes this work tricky. As human beings, we tend to seek similarities and reject differences. Similarities provide emotional security. Differences are threatening. One way people tend to deal with differences is to stereotype, attack and create *one up/one down* power relationships (Weisbord & Janoff, 2007). Think how often you see this in individuals, groups, organizations, communities and societies around the planet. Our challenge as social scientists is to enable systems to overcome the impulse to deny, ignore or blur differences and default to silos, fragmenting and scapegoating.

Why differentiation and integration can make a difference

It is not easy to overcome our initial response to differences. We are wired to be wary. As I said, most leaders strategize with the *usual* people. It is frustrating to have to stop and listen to those who do not see the world as we do. But there is a cost to comfort. One person cannot change a whole system. Systems are just too big, too diverse, the power in them is too widely distributed and things are moving too fast. When leaders include people with diverse perspectives and bring all experiences to bear, they open opportunities for people to unlock themselves from fixed positions, see themselves as part of the larger whole and discover creative solutions. That is systems-integration – getting the differentiated viewpoints articulated so they can find a shared way forward (Weisbord & Janoff, 2015).

The Future Search approach

With D/I as our theory for systems change, Marvin Weisbord (see marvin-weisbord.com) and I started working together not long after he completed the first edition of his groundbreaking book, *Productive Workplaces* (1987, 2004, 2012). Even then the world was turbulent, which called for thinking beyond traditional ways of change. Marv's research addressed a way to enable diverse people to create new structures and policies that reflect the fast-changing environment. He formulated "everybody improving whole systems" as his practice-theory for change.

Marv and I developed Future Search (http://futuresearch.net) as a methodology to apply "everybody improving whole systems". We articulated four design principles: (1) Get the whole system in the room, those with authority, resources, expertise, information, and those impacted by the outcomes. (2) Enable participants to understand the whole of the system – internal forces, external forces and the relationship between the two. (3) Focus on the future and common ground by putting the problems and conflicts in the background and what people are ready, willing and able to do in the foreground. (4) Enable participants to take responsibility for themselves and their action. We also built a methodology, as shown in http://futuresearch.net/about/methodology/. We used these design principles and our methodology with large diverse groups to create conditions where stakeholders from within and outside the system could differentiate their perspectives, create a shared vision and act together.

Applying Future Search Principles

For decades, Future Searches have been bringing these principles to life in a three-day innovative strategic-planning meeting. Marv and I co-wrote the first edition of *Future Search* in 1995 and have updated it based on real experiences of Future Search Network colleagues (Weisbord & Janoff, 2010). Participants, diverse in function and demographics, explore their past, get deeply into their present reality, create preferred futures, converge their learning and discover a common ground agenda they translate into action. We believe that, for a system to change, people have to interact with people who are part of their environment and key to their success. When the same people talk to each other, they perpetuate the kind of condition they are trying to get out from under. D/I theory tells us: you can't integrate unless you have first differentiated! (For illustrations of Future Searches in Action see http://futuresearch.net/resources/booksandvideos.)

By diversity we mean people with different stakes, different roles, different perspectives, different experiences, those within the boundaries of the system and those outside, those who have always had a voice and those who have not, those who have always had access and those who have not, demographic and geographic diversity that reflects the whole of the system

… and, when it applies, young people! A note on involving young people: Many planners have challenged the idea of including young people in a three-day meeting of adults. It is a lovely surprise when people see the benefit of learning, first-hand, the views of the next generation. In the following paragraphs I share examples of Future Searches that involved young people and the issues they helped reveal.

Future searches show how social and economic issues are inextricably linked!

When Marv and I met with residents of Santa Cruz County, CA we learned how a serious housing problem had become a community crisis. ("Discovering Community" video at https://futuresearch.net/resources/booksandvideos/). When the population of the area increased dramatically, housing needs exploded while housing prices soared. A recession had people unemployed and an earthquake exacerbated the problem. Residents on fixed incomes could no longer afford to live there. The community was in dire need for affordable housing and years of meetings with housing leadership had not produced a plan that had community support. In our planning we broadened the scope from a housing focus to a community focus, since housing links to every segment. This allowed the planners to include a broad section of their community (and young people) in a Future Search for a shared appreciation of Santa Cruz County and the housing dilemma.

The struggle during the meeting was potent as we could hear in the participants' actual words. "If we already have affordable housing in our neighborhood, we don't want more". "I face a whole group of different people needing housing every day, look at them, living in garages". The dialogue deepened and emerged with this commitment, "We don't have to solve this, we just have to agree these are two needs that have to be addressed as we build this plan". Marv and I call this the integrating statement and when it was voiced, we knew the community had the capacity to move forward. They were ready to confirm their common ground agenda and take action. D/I theory in practice. Not only did they unlock housing plans that had been deadlocked, but they also found they could act together on a wide range of linking concerns like jobs for displaced workers, business expansion, literacy education and equity and inclusion. Why? Those stakeholders had been in the room and present to each other.

Future searches reinforce that who is in the room matters!

IKEA is the world's largest home-furnishings company and has always had a commitment to sustainability (Weisbord & Janoff, 2010). When Marv and

I met the top leaders in 2008, they had not been able to put sustainability into a strategic context. "We had been thinking about the environmental question, but didn't have a common language across the whole organization. We lacked a holistic view", said Torbjorn Loof, then head of IKEA's design, production and distribution arm. IKEA wanted to integrate sustainability internally in their business processes, and more, externally in their impact with customers and suppliers around the world. To take this step, they brought together their internal leaders, co-workers from all functions, their customers, suppliers and other external partners, such as World Wildlife Fund and UNICEF. In three days together they struggled with the obvious tension between profitability and sustainability.

One reason leaders rarely bring these views into one room is they assume the environmentalists will put sustainability over profit and big business will put profit over the environment. That perception was real in 2008 and may still be real today. But, in this meeting, they discovered shared values. An environmental voice stood out at one point, "We *need* you to be profitable, and we can figure out how we can do both". Their breakthroughs came in a shared commitment to a long-range "cradle-to-cradle" concept of materials, design and production. Every function and process throughout the company went on to implement their own sustainability goals in line with the common ground agenda. People and Planet Positive, IKEA's name for its sustainability strategy, continues to transform their business, all of the industries in the IKEA value chain and life at home for people around the world.

Gathering this diversity on a complex economic, technical and environmental issue, such as supply chain sustainability, took vision and courage. Bringing in customers, suppliers and external stakeholders was unconventional, but had a huge payoff. While this takes many leaders out of their comfort zone, the question a leader must ask is, "Can I really afford the privilege of comfort, and risk staying stuck or failing?"

How to make a tangible difference on global climate change

We must now talk about climate change, our planet's most pressing problem. I believe every whole system's change initiative must bring our climate crisis into the conversation, whatever the focus. If any system does not think climate change is relevant, they have missed the point. Here is an example of how climate surfaced because of who was present. The Archbishop of the Church of Sweden initiated a movement to create a more welcoming Europe for people on the move. Those gathered in the Future Search included grassroots practitioners, policy makers and refugees from

15 European countries. The focus was on identifying the most serious issues for refugees and possible steps ahead. "It was three days of hard work and intense conversations, mapping our common history, identifying our most pressing concerns and seeking ways to move forward together" said one participant. At the same time, there was no escaping the impact of climate on these refugees. In most of their home countries, droughts and floods have impacted natural resources causing food and employment scarcity, destabilized economies, violence and persecution. Immigrants are victims of climate change as much as the terrorist regimes they are fleeing. There is no magic solution to climate change, but a denial is no longer an option, therefore, whatever the scale, from awareness to mitigation to policy change, we must keep the issue alive (www.aworldofneighbours.com/pre-summit -keeping-our-humanity/).

In another meeting, titled *Youth 2030!* a diverse group of adults and 60 young people from across Sweden gathered to meet the opportunities and challenges of a "new Sweden". This phrase refers to Sweden having admitted more refugees per capita than any other country in Europe. The Future Search focus was on building a future for young people, some of whom are first- and second-generation Swedes. While their concerns highlighted the particular needs of youth – education, mental health, safety, meeting places – one young man made it clear there was no future for him or his peers if the adults didn't address climate straight on. "Many young people think about this. It affects our sense of security and hope". He was a student at Globala Gymnasiet, a high school for students with an interest in global issues, so he brought a broad perspective. His contribution informed the action planning. The sponsoring organization, Fryshuset, and their partners built sustainability into their agendas. An extraordinary outcome, recently announced and due in large part to the meeting, is the unique collaboration of Fryshuset and Greenpeace called Climate Changemakerspaces. It promotes youth engagement in environmental, climate and justice related issues and centers around tools, platforms and networks for youth. With physical and digital venues in six countries around the world, this spectacular project will undoubtedly turn young people's anxieties, passions and energy for a crisis-free world into concrete actions that will make a difference (https://fryshuset.se/nyhet /fryshuset-and-greenpeace-in-collaboration-to-support-youths-engage- ment-in-climate/).

It is too late to get ahead of many climate issues. Extreme weather, food insecurity and migration are here now. But the problems we have created will be around forever if we do not step up our efforts. Including stakeholders with a sustainability perspective in every community and organization planning meeting will show how serious we are about climate. Challenging ourselves to look this crisis in the face, at every level, is the way out of the mess. We must leverage our role as social scientists.

Social scientists must be courageous!

Leaders are asking for guidance. Who are they asking? They are asking us – consultants, applied social scientists, scholar practitioners, facilitators, hosts, advisors, thought partners, system's specialists, process experts – whatever we call ourselves. The requests are: *Help us solve these wicked problems! We need systems that are responsive! Help us find solutions to get us out of the mess we are in! We want to create a safer, healthier future!* Our leverage is in the trust we build as we support leaders to have the courage to do something new. They have the authority to get the right people together. We have the art and science of systems change. When we hold the integrity of our beliefs and support their courage with our own, we are doing the world a great service.

What social scientists must do

We know it is not easy and pushback is inevitable, but this is not the time to compromise. When we are with clients who want to gather top leaders to make strategic decisions, guide them toward including more stakeholders! When we are with clients who want to shorten the time, but expect creative solutions, be honest about the sacrifice! Creativity requires three things: time, space and permission. When you compress the time, people share what they already know. New ideas come from slowing down and listening. The environment matters too, so pay attention to creating a conducive working space. Then, give others, and yourself, permission to be on a journey of discovery, rather than aim for predictable outcomes. These, to me, are conditions to which we must commit if we want breakthroughs. Mostly, we must bring different voices into the planning, including those on the "they won't come" list. If we don't push these boundaries, systems will stay broken. Let us not forget – bringing large groups of people together to build community is a worthy step. But gathering *only* decision makers or *only* those impacted by the decisions bypasses our urgent need to change the structures and policies creating the problems in the first place (Janoff, 2016).

My big ask!

Discovering common ground has been a mantra for Marv and me since the 1990s. It is now a common phrase. Putting it to practice is what I and my Future Search Network colleagues around the world do every time we do this work. We never take for granted a diverse group of people will discover a shared future, but we do believe, under the right conditions, the probability is high. And, if there is no common ground, that too will be clearer. After thousands of experiences, previously fragmented communities of people have discovered solutions to tough problems. Trust me, once you hear a participant say, "Well, we are all here and if we do not solve this, no one else will", you will never short change a planning process again.

So, what do I mean by social scientists standing together? Each of us can influence transformative change by embedding the principle of "everybody improving whole systems". We can stand for bringing together people with differences that make a difference. We can respect that learning takes time when we are crossing boundaries that had kept us apart. We can live in the uncertainty of not knowing what we will discover, until we discover it. This will enrich everyone's understanding of these crises, expand our possibilities for action and offer hope. It will always be a struggle because, remember, we humans do not like to deal with differences. But as social scientists we value tough conversations that can lead to new ways of thinking, Our role is to reassure leaders that differences are our resources and a journey of discovery will lead to unpredictable, constructive outcomes. Creating conditions that enable people to move toward wholeness, step into the unknown, struggle and find ways out of darkness is a privilege!

That is the message about which we should make a loud noise. Then maybe, just maybe, together, we can bring these crises down to a manageable level and build a world where we, and those who follow, can breathe the air, drink the water, live in safety, grow up healthy and experience tolerance, fairness and compassion.

References

Agazarian, Y. M. (1997). *Systems-centered theory for groups*. New York: The Guilford Press.

Bohm, D. (1996). *On dialogue*. Ed. Lee Nichol. New York: Routledge.

Janoff, S. (2016). My future search journey. *OD Practitioner*, *48*(1), 48–50.

Von Bertalanffy, L. (1952). *General systems theory*. New York: Wiley.

Weisbord, M. R., & Janoff, S. (2007). *Don't just do something, stand there! Ten principles for leading meetings that matter*. Oakland, CA: Berrett-Koehler.

Weisbord, M. R. (2012). *Productive workplaces: Dignity, meaning and community in the 21st century* (3rd ed.). San Francisco, CA: Jossey-Bass.

Weisbord, M. R., & Janoff, S. (2010). *Future search: Getting the whole system in the room for vision, commitment and action* (3rd ed.). Oakland, CA: Berrett-Koehler.

Weisbord, M. R., & Janoff, S. (2015). *Lead more, control less: Eight advanced leadership skills that overturn convention!* San Francisco, CA: Berrett-Koehler.

3 The important role of management researchers in addressing global crises

Insights from Innovation North

Pratima (Tima) Bansal and Garima Sharma

The frequency and magnitude of global crises, such as climate change induced weather events, pandemics, financial shocks and civil unrest, are growing. Although many of these crises are catalyzed by business, the public discourse about these is dominated by 'experts' from climate science, epidemiology, economics and political science – not from business schools.

The absence of management researchers in these public conversations does not mean that management researchers have been completely silent. Instead, management researchers are playing a unique role by creating private spaces in which managers can reflect and act, not only learn and understand. Such exchanges are important in addressing global crises.

In this chapter, we describe this type of knowledge creation through an initiative that we launched in 2019, called Innovation North. This initiative provides a space for managers and researchers to co-create knowledge that can help managers innovate for turbulent environments. This initiative develops insights that serve a dual purpose: (1) for *managers* to understand, organize for, and deflect crises, and (2) for *researchers* to understand innovation processes that create value for themselves and society over the long term.

In this essay, we first describe the lab at Innovation North. We argue that the approach taken by this lab is particularly suited for systems-based global crises. A global crisis is a systems crisis if it disrupts the way in which communities of people live, work and interact. A systems crisis is particularly insidious because its effects are unpredictable and potentially catastrophic – much as we saw with COVID-19. A systems view asks actors to see not just their own perspective, but the broader system, so that they are able to adapt to and potentially mitigate crises. After we describe the lab, we show how the lab's epistemological foundations are grounded in American Pragmatism. This approach seeks not only for science-based understanding

DOI: 10.4324/9781003109372-4

of global crises, but a type of knowledge that stimulates reflection and action. We hope this chapter will inspire social science researchers to engage actively with managers to address global crises.

Innovation North: Innovating the corporate innovation process

Bansal launched Innovation North in October 2019. Its ambition was to develop the knowledge and practices needed for organizations to *innovate products and services that create value for business and society simultaneously for the long term.* Innovation North seeks several outcomes to address this challenge: (a) to *co-create knowledge* that is both rigorous and relevant so that it can be used by both managers and researchers; (b) to *catalyze action* by companies that can serve as inspiration for other companies and test cases for researchers; and (c) to *build a network of partnerships* in which individuals can call on others, but also form collaborations that tackle systems challenges.

Bansal created Innovation North because businesses were both experiencing and inadvertently catalyzing systems-based crises. Managers, however, did not have the tools or knowledge to understand how to manage within them.

Contemporary corporate innovation research and practice are either directed at business challenges tackled by for-profit businesses or societal challenges tackled by non-profit organizations. Business innovation processes include stage-gate models, design thinking and open innovation (Brown, 2008; Chesbrough, 2003; Cooper, 1990). These processes generate value for business, but can inadvertently catalyze global crises, such as the increased traffic congestion caused by Uber or the social consequences of the gig economy (Dubal & Whittaker, 2020). Non-profit social innovation processes, on the other hand, tackle societal challenges, such as traffic congestion and social instability, but the solutions do not offer a business case, so that for-profit businesses are unlikely to adopt the solutions.

Innovation North co-creates academically rigorous and practically relevant knowledge with researchers and managers through a lab process. It will mobilize that knowledge through open-source digital media and develop communities of practice and training programs. Innovation North's lab kicked off in October 2019 and will wind down in July 2024.

The lab draws on Bansal and Sharma's previous experiences with the Network for Business Sustainability (Sharma & Bansal, in press; 2020) and the experiences of the Minnesota Innovation Research Project (Van de Ven & Poole, 1990). Innovation North also applies the principles of American pragmatism through action research (Eden & Huxham, 1996) and engaged scholarship (Van de Ven, 2007).

The lab participants come from various sectors forming a system of actors and issues within the lab. Specifically, there are three main categories of participants involved in the lab: (1) managers, (2) researchers, and (3) students. The *managers* involve two people each from 25 participating organizations. At least one of the managers must be a senior executive who handles the innovation budget to ensure that the insights from the lab are mobilized within the participating organization. We intentionally invited managers from a diverse group of cross-sectoral (for-profits, non-profits and government), non-competitive organizations to foster an open, sharing environment and build a network of organizations that can change systems within Canada. The *researchers* are faculty members interested in innovation and systems change. A regular group of five faculty members participate in the lab, along with a small group of postdoctoral fellows and doctoral students. In addition, we invite two to three *undergraduate students* to join each session so that they can share some of their key insights more broadly.

The lab sessions are held quarterly. The first two sessions in October 2019 and January 2020 were held in person in Toronto. Subsequent sessions transitioned online because of the COVID-19 pandemic. Each session is animated by a keynote provocateur, who has a faculty appointment, has demonstrated thought leadership and can speak to managers. The keynote provocateurs have included Peter Senge (MIT), Otto Scharmer (MIT), Terry Irwin (Carnegie Mellon), Kristel van Ael (Antwerp), Jorrit de Jong (Harvard) and Melanie Goodchild (Waterloo). The lab organizers are from the Ivey Business School and MaRS, a social innovation lab in Toronto. They design each lab session as a unique event, addressing a topic chosen by participants. Depending on the keynote provocateur's skills, the session may involve short lectures with breakout groups, case studies or the application of innovation design tools. The researchers facilitate the breakout groups, while also studying the interactions among participants. In some cases, the lab organizers are deeply involved in designing the lab session; in others, the keynote prefers to guide the session.

Sample lab session

On July 30, 2020, Kristel van Ael, an assistant professor at the University of Antwerp and a Partner at the design agency, Namahn, presented two tools from her Systemic Design Toolkit (www.systemicdesigntoolkit.org). Van Ael had applied the toolkit to societal challenges that require systems solutions, such as helping an NGO address discrimination and racism in Brussels. She had limited experience applying these tools to business, who care more about firm-level value than systems-level challenges. *A priori,* the researchers and managers did not have experience with the tools, nor did they know how to use them in a corporate context.

Working with van Ael in the months leading up to the session, Bansal and postdoctoral fellow, Angela Greco, developed an exercise that offered participants an opportunity to apply two of the tools to a specific challenge confronting one of the lab participants, and relevant to others. The lab was designed to build a community of learners who could help solve each other's innovation challenges, while building knowledge together. The exercise required lab participants to take the role of a CEO tasked to build a robot by integrating technologies from various providers (sensors, cloud computing, mechanical aspects). The solution would require collaboration among different actors within the industrial ecosystem.

The first tool asked participants to map the flows among five different "actants", which can include human and non-human actors, in the system. These actants included the company wanting to find a robotic solution, an auto manufacturer that would buy the technology, a technology company that would provide sensors, an academic with specific knowledge and an employee. The material flows helped to show interdependencies and opportunities.

Once the participants identified actants' interests and the respective material flows, the participants applied a second tool that asked them to analyze the paradox between cooperation and competition. If the participants were too collaborative, then it was likely that one actant was making too quick a compromise and offering too many resources to the other. Yet, if participants were too competitive, the collaboration would fail, making them all worse off. By putting the collaborative–competitive paradox in full view, participants could zoom out to see the whole system and the total resources that could be generated through the collaboration and then determine how to distribute the resources equitably. In that way, all actants were better off.

Bansal and Greco adapted the tools by drawing upon their academic knowledge of systems, innovation and paradox. As well, the participating managers provided the details for Bansal and Greco to adapt the tools. In juxtaposing their academic knowledge with the participating organization's concrete problem details, Bansal and Greco adapted the tools by focusing on what is useful for a community of inquirers, rather than privileging academic knowledge.

The participants engaged in "pragmatic experimentation" (Wicks & Freeman, 1998), by applying the tools to understand how business can innovate through collaboration. By applying the tools in small groups, and then debriefing together, participants took away relevant insights for systemic innovation, which they expressed would be relevant in changing their organization's innovation process. In subsequent interviews with the lab participants, researchers explored what was useful about these tools and what could be improved, drawing on the participants' experience to refine the tools for a broader community beyond the lab participants.

The larger group of researchers observing the lab session made a number of important observations, such as the importance of including civil society and the natural environment as actants. They also observed how difficult it was for managers to see a systems solution, until they started to talk explicitly about paradoxes. The researchers used these insights to improve the lab design further. The researchers are also using these insights as prospective data for building a theory of systems change and innovation. Further, Bansal, Greco and another lab researcher (Mazi Raz) applied the tool to a classroom setting and adapted it further, so the tools could be shared with other business school professors who seek to apply paradox thinking to tackle the challenges in fostering collaboration. The materials are distributed through Ivey Publishing.

The pragmatic foundations of Innovation North

The lab draws upon the principles of American Pragmatism (Dewey, 1910; James, 1907), which is particularly suited for systems-based global crises. A science-based paradigm seeks to model the environment, but such modeling is difficult for complex socio-technical systems that are being disrupted. Several scholars have distilled and applied pragmatic principles to organizational studies (e.g., Evans, 2000; Farjoun, Ansell, & Boin, 2015; Martela, 2015; Simpson & den Hond, 2021). These principles shape the epistemological foundations of the lab. We describe the two main principles we draw from and their applications to the lab.

First, pragmatism presumes that reality cannot be fully known, and the process of learning within a community of inquirers shapes what is known (Dewey, 1908). Reality is particularly difficult to model in complex dynamic systems and the outcomes are particularly difficult to predict. Pragmatism, especially from Dewey's perspective, is unabashed about social change (Martela, 2015). It focuses on experimentation for figuring out 'what is useful', as defined by the community, rather than researchers independently and objectively developing models that are carefully tested for their efficacy but may not speak directly to managers' realities (Wicks & Freeman, 1998).

As a result, learning and insights through a pragmatic lens do not lie solely in the analysis of historical data, but rather in narratives of what can or will be. Pragmatism focuses both on retrospective knowledge as well as prospective knowledge (Weick, 1999). Dewey called this a shift from "antecedently real" to knowledge needed to "deal with problems as they arise" (Dewey, 1988: 14). From this paradigm, the knower, context and knowledge are deeply entangled. One begets the other, so that knowledge is constantly being shaped and reshaped through practice. A pragmatic approach to knowledge, then, relies not only on scientific concepts and models, but also on the tools and frameworks, such as Porter's Five Forces or Design Thinking, that are tools for solving problems by evoking reflection and action (Evans, 2000).

We drew on these ideas to design Innovation North into a space for prospective solution making. Instead of providing the answers from existing concepts and knowledge, the lab introduces the participants to tools and frameworks that foster knowing by doing. Further, these tools are ideas in the making. They are presumed to be always incomplete, rather than static bearers of "truth". Dewey describes such an approach as one in which knowledge is the "settled outcome of inquiry" (Dewey, 1941: 175) for a community of inquirers, rather than a thing that exists with *a priori* certainty and can be discovered.

A second important principle of pragmatism is that it values both experiential, concrete knowledge and theoretical, abstract knowledge. It challenges the pursuit of rationality if it is at the expense of imagination (Alexander, 1990), which is why assembling practitioners with researchers in the lab offers a powerful mix of co-creating knowledge that imbricates the concrete with the abstract, the experiential with the theoretical, and rationality with imagination. Practitioners seek ideas or concepts that can help them solve problems, and address perplexities, such as those related to global systems-based crises. At the same time, practitioners' experiences can provide "organizational scientists with grist for the theoretical mill" (Astley & Zammuto, 1992: 454), such that researchers can build new "skyhooks" (Ohmann, 1955 cited by Astley & Zammuto, 1992) to help practitioners climb to the other side of organizational challenges.

James (1907: 9) combines the two worlds of research and practice to conceive of collective inquiry as,

> [y]ou want a system that will combine both things, the scientific loyalty to facts and willingness to take account of them, the spirit of adaptation and accommodation, in short, but also the old confidence in human values and the resultant spontaneity.

By co-creating knowledge, researchers can generate new questions and expand their theoretical enterprises (Schulz & Nicolai, 2015), and managers can see beyond the immediate crisis to not only learn from previous crises but also prevent future ones.

The lab fosters such co-creation in a few ways. In applying the tools and frameworks introduced in the lab, participants experience what Dewey describes as doubts or breakdowns (Van de Ven, 2007) when their lived experience may not match their experiences in applying the tools. This breakdown is followed by a process of abduction, in which the community of inquirers, the lab participants in our case, generate possible options to address the breakdown, i.e., "new hypotheses are generated to combine the nonroutine with existing knowledge, which can lead to new beliefs and habits as well as imaginative leaps" (Farjoun et al., 2015: 5). Such a process fosters revision in the tools to make them useful for other "communities of inquirers" beyond the lab, helping us pursue "practical and local solutions rather than grand theoretical agendas" (Simpson & den Hond, 2021: 11). As well, researchers, as part of the lab, study the lab processes and continuously refine the processes, generating knowledge that combines facts, human values and spontaneity.

Researchers and managers collaborating to deflect systems-based global crises

Innovation North illustrates a new way in which researchers and managers can come together to co-create knowledge. Our goal is to help managers see the system, use tools based on rigor and relevance, and develop managers' capacity for systems thinking that they can apply to their innovation processes, so they solve not only their own organizational challenges, but also societal challenges.

What Innovation North also shows is that knowledge co-creation happens in many ways. It is not just about imbricating academic and practical knowledge but also integrating complementary skills, such as the academic skills of critiquing assumptions and seeing narrative arcs with the practitioners' skills of application and thought experimentation. Specifically, the lab sessions permit the keynote provocateur, researchers and managers to dialogue around abstract ideas to make them concrete. Managers make these abstract ideas relevant to their own work (Astley & Zammuto, 1992), in turn providing insights to the academics for improving the tools and synthesizing the concepts.

We believe that this process of co-creating knowledge lies uniquely in the domain of management researchers. This 'research' process can address the significant global crises that threaten society. This approach to knowledge co-creation should be recognized as not only a legitimate exercise, but also a necessary approach to management research.

References

Alexander, T. M. (1990). *Pragmatic imagination*. Transactions of the Charles S. Perice Society.

Astley, W. G., & Zammuto, R. F. (1992). Organization science, managers, and language games. *Organization Science, 3*(4), 443–460.

Brown, T. (2008). Design thinking. *Harvard Business Review, 86*(6), 84.

Chesbrough, H. W. (2003). *Open innovation: The new imperative for creating and profiting from technology.* Boston, MA: Harvard Business School Press.

Cooper, R. G. (1990). Stage-gate systems: A new tool for managing new products. *Business Horizons, 33*(3), 44–54.

Dewey, J. (1908). What does pragmatism mean by practical? *Journal of Philosophy, Psychology and Scientific Methods, 5*, 85–99.

Dewey, J. (1910). *How we think.* Lexington, MA: Heath & Co.

Dewey, J. (1929). *The quest for certainty: A study of the relation of knowledge and action.* New York, NY: Minton, Balch & Co.

Dewey, J. (1941). Propositions, warranted assertibility, and truth. *The Journal of Philosophy, 38*(7), 169–186.

Dubal, V., & Whittaker, M. (2020, March 25). Uber drivers are being forced to choose between risking Covid-19 or starvation. *The Guardian.* Retrieved from https://www.theguardian.com/technology/2020/mar/25/uber-lyft-gig-economy -coronavirus.

Eden, C., & Huxham, C. (1996). Action research for management research. *British Journal of Management, 7*, 75–86.

Evans, K. G. (2000). Reclaiming John Dewey. *Administration & Society, 32*(3), 308–328.

Farjoun, M., Ansell, C., & Boin, A. (2015). PERSPECTIVE—Pragmatism in organization studies: Meeting the challenges of a dynamic and complex world. *Organization Science, 26*(6), 1553–1804.

James, W. (1907). *Pragmatism: A new name for some old ways of thinking.* New York: Longman Green & Co.

Martela, F. (2015). Fallible inquiry with ethical ends-in-view: A pragmatist philosophy of science for organizational research. *Organization Studies, 36*(4), 537–563.

Ohmann, O. A. (1955). Skyhooks. *Harvard Business Review.*

Schulz, A. -c., & Nicolai, A. T. (2015). The intellectual link between management research and popularization media: A bibliometric analysis of the Harvard Business Review. *Academy of Management Learning & Education, 14*(1), 31–49.

Sharma, G., & Bansal, P. (2020). Cocreating rigorous and relevant knowledge. *Academy of Management Journal, 63*(2).

Sharma, G., & Bansal, P. (In press). Partnering up: Including managers as research partners in systematic reviews. *Organizational Research Methods.* doi:10.1177/1094428120965706.

Simpson, B., & den Hond, F. (2021). The contemporary resonances of classical pragmatism for studying organization and organizing. *Organization Studies.* https://doi.org/10.1177/0170840621991689.

Van de Ven, A. H. (2007). *Engaged scholarship: A guide for organizational and social research.* Oxford; New York: Oxford University Press.

Van de Ven, A. H., & Poole, M. S. (1990). Methods for studying innovation development in the Minnesota Innovation Research Program. *Organization Science*, *1*(3), 313–335.

Weick, K. E. (1999). That's moving: Theories that matter. *Journal of Management Inquiry*, *8*(2), 134–142.

Wicks, A. C., & Freeman, R. E. (1998). Organization studies and the new pragmatism: Positivism, anti-positivism, and the search for ethics. *Organization Science*, *9*(2), 123–251.

4 Dialogic Organization Development and the Generative Change Model

Opportunities and challenges for managing global crises

Gervase R. Bushe and Robert J. Marshak

The challenge

Dialogic Organization Development (OD) methods (Bushe & Marshak, 2009, 2015a) emerged over the past 30 years to aid organizations and leaders in addressing increasingly complex (Snowden, 2002) adaptive challenges (Heifetz, 1998). These are problems with many moving parts, known and unknown interdependencies, that span multiple boundaries and require changes in behavior and changes in attitudes, perceptions and cognitive maps of stakeholders. Successful cases of Dialogic OD in large group settings of hundreds or even thousands of participants (e.g., Cooperrider, 2012; Davies, 1992; Lukensmeyer, 2015) appear to follow what we have described, building on the dialogic approach, as the Generative Change Model (Bushe, 2020; Marshak & Bushe, 2018).

Global crises such as global warming, the Covid-19 pandemic and mass migrations fit the kinds of issues for which generative approaches to change are designed. In a few cases a generative change approach has been successfully used for community and social issues. However, there are crucial differences between organizations and communities that, to our knowledge, have not been reckoned with to produce reliably successful generative change processes at the community, let alone global, level. This chapter will briefly describe Dialogic OD, and then the Generative Change Model and why it is more effective for managing complex, adaptive challenges than more traditional planned change approaches. We also describe two challenges we believe need to be addressed for generative change processes to be used successfully for global issues. While these challenges apply to all change situations regardless of size, they are particularly vexing when dealing with scales larger than organizations.

DOI: 10.4324/9781003109372-5

What is Dialogic OD?

In parallel with the increasingly complex and uncertain contexts and challenges organizations face have been the advancement and application of new ideas from the social sciences. While offering new insights and approaches to social change, they also suggest a less controllable, more ambiguous, world calling for letting go of long established and culturally reinforced notions of command-and-control leadership in favor of newer approaches. These newer approaches, like Appreciative Inquiry, Future Search and Open Space Technology utilize recent advances in social science (social construction) and natural science (complex adaptive systems and emergence) and have been used in various contexts to address social and global concerns. These are exciting developments that hold great promise for the challenges of contemporary times.

Recently, to help clarify and define what's different about these newer approaches to change, we labeled them as "Dialogic OD". It's important to understand that Dialogic OD is not simply about dialogue or prescribing ways in which people ought to talk and listen. We selected that title to contrast this set of practices with more conventional "Diagnostic OD" approaches to change. We also selected that label because all the different methods we classify as dialogic practices agree that transformational change occurs by changing the ongoing conversations and resulting meaning-making that have become patterned and routinized in the subject organization.

In studying the underlying similarities in dozens of different dialogic methodologies we have concluded "that it is not the method, but the mindset of leaders and change agents" that makes the change process more or less transformational (Bushe & Marshak, 2014, 2016). The contours of this mindset include premises that invite leaders and change agents to move away from traditional problem-solving, analyze and envision, top-down, directive, thinking and doing (Bushe & Marshak, 2015b). Instead, we find processes that are purpose driven, focus on preferred futures, engage those who must change in deciding on those changes and utilize self-organizing, generative and emergent social processes are more transformational.

Part of that mindset includes the belief that transformational change requires at least one of the following three enablers. These are (1) a shared narrative about the nature of the organization and/or the presenting challenge is changed; (2) a disruption to current processes of organizing in a way that stimulates self-organization and the emergence of new, better and adapted processes and (3) the use of a generative image that creates opportunities for new conversations, thoughts and actions (Bushe & Marshak, 2014, 2015b).

The Generative Change Model

One strand of Dialogic OD uses large group interventions that can involve hundreds of participants, utilizing dialogic methods and mindsets to produce rapid transformational change. This "Generative Change Model" is broad enough that it encompasses a wide variety of different methods, specific enough that its use can be imagined by people who are only used to planned change methods, and revealing enough that it alerts leaders and change agents to important considerations for the successful utilization of Dialogic OD methods.

A generative change process begins when a complex, adaptive challenge has been identified and accepted as requiring attention by leaders willing to sponsor the change. Leaders and change agents then reframe it in a way that will capture the interest and engagement of the diverse stakeholders who must ultimately generate, embrace and enact the thinking and actions needed for transformational change. The most powerful purpose statements are "generative images", a combination of a few words or even a new metaphor that are both appealing but ambiguous, and open up opportunities for new conversations and new ideas (Bushe, 2020; Bushe & Storch, 2015). The purpose statement is used to engage the people who will have to change into joining one or more events designed to produce "generative conversations" – conversations that will lead to new ideas people want to act on. These are normally events involving large groups of participants designed to include the diversity of stakeholders, deepen the group's understanding of the systemic nature of the issues, allow people with similar interests and ideas to find each other, and ultimately launch as many pilot projects as possible, with basic guardrails articulated by organizational leaders. At the end of these events participants are encouraged to take initiative and act on their ideas without waiting for permission. Processes for monitoring what then takes place allow leaders to learn from the pilots, support promising initiatives and scale up and embed successful ones. Figure 4.1 depicts the Generative Change Model.

Recently, Bushe (2020) illustrated the use of the Generative Change Model to transform an old, unionized warehouse and distribution department with 170 employees inside a company with depots distributed across a large geographic area. The adaptive challenge the leaders wanted to address was increasing employee engagement throughout the department and reducing the daily sense of chaos. The chaos was caused by an antiquated IT system slated to be replaced at some unknown time in the future and employees responding to demands from other parts of the organization in ways that circumvented procedures, creating even more chaos. Leadership was concerned about poor morale that resulted from the perception that a

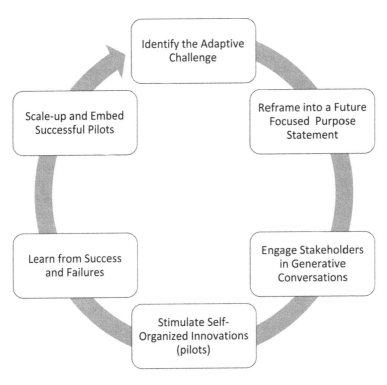

Figure 4.1 The Generative Change Model (Bushe, 2020)

good day was one where you didn't get yelled at by a customer. The generative image they developed for their purpose was "stress-free customer service" and began with a one-day event where all the managers, supervisors and some volunteers from the unionized workforce (about 60 people in total) resulted in 13 self-initiated pilot projects. It was widely viewed as a new way to do things and successful. As leaders tracked what was taking place, they realized four of the pilots were complex and interrelated. They made the champions of those four pilots into a design team that organized another two-day event with the purpose of "ensuring depots get their last order before they have to make their next order". They engaged volunteers from all the departments and the whole warehouse staff in exploring how to reduce turnaround, from the time materials were requested to the time they were shipped, from three days to one. Seventeen pilots emerged from that event, and they reached their turnaround reduction goals in six weeks. The impact of experiencing successful self-organizing, emergent change by workers, along with a change in shared narratives about what employees could do, led to real cultural changes that many years later continue to make this department the model of an adaptive, engaged workforce even though all the managers who led this project have since been promoted. Furthermore, by nurturing and amplifying a pilot focused on how to log in information at the warehouse, leaders were able to engage the entire organization in going from a pencil-and-paper-based system to a fully modern, digital barcode and scanner operation. This transformation occurred in less than 18 months without a plan, a vision, training or a dedicated budget. Instead, they did it through a generative change process.

Another example of generative change in the medical field involved developing a new regional strategy for managing cancer care in Sweden. The regional cancer center leader adopted a deliberatively vague and open process while avoiding the top-down implementation of a single blueprint. The change effort was greatly influenced by the leader's support for the adoption of a metaphor that emerged and served as a generative image for the entire effort. That generative image was of an aqueduct that delivered effective care processes through its horizontal dimensions around the patient while also needing robust supporting dimensions underneath. This image of an ambidextrous healthcare system broke with the traditional bureaucratic model that pervaded this healthcare sector. It provided a new perspective that shaped subsequent conversations, thinking and behaviors, leading to many successful patient care innovations (Huzzard, Hellström, & Lifvergren, 2014).

There are several things that make the generative change approach significantly different from traditional planned change. One is a focus on preferred futures rather than a focus on solving problems. Another is the use of a common purpose embraced by a diversity of stakeholders to drive the change process, instead of a strategic vision articulated by the leader. A third is widespread engagement in generative conversations by the stakeholders who will have to change in devising the actual changes, rather than mostly the engagement of experts and authorities. Still another is use of numerous experiments and pilot projects to learn as you go about potential adaptive moves rather than first agreeing on and then implementing a preferred comprehensive solution. Research on organizational change (Bushe & Kassam, 2005; Hastings & Schwarz, 2019; Mirabeau & Maguire, 2014; Rowland & Higgs, 2008) and experience in the field consistently demonstrate that generative change produces more change, more quickly than planned change approaches.

Generative change appears to offer considerable opportunities for leaders and change agents to design effective responses to global crises, and indeed, there are instances where we see what looks like a generative change approach being used. More and less successful examples include most of the Earth Summits, the Paris Climate Accords, Walmart's transformation of its global supply chain to net carbon neutral (Spicer & Hyatt, 2017), increasing environmental conservation in Pakistan (Schwass, 1992) and attempts to bring peace to the world through the United Religions Initiative (Finegold, Holland, & Lingham, 2002).

Two challenges when using generative change methods to address societal problems

When seeking to apply a dialogic mindset and generative change method to address global problems, important differences between organizations and larger social entities like communities, nations and the world need to be recognized. There are many examples of attempts to use large group interventions and a dialogic mindset to address community, national and international issues, but with mixed results. Often the good intentions and high spirits produced by dialogic events fade away without much tangible change. Two important issues need to be worked through to use these methods and mindset reliably and successfully at scale. These are the need for sponsorship and ensuring that emergent self-organized changes will be good for the collective, what we will call convivial emergence.

Sponsorship

Sponsors are the public and private sector leaders with the authority and resources to make the changes in structures, processes, policies, etc., needed for adaptive change. In the Generative Change Model sponsors are important at the beginning in framing the purpose and supporting efforts and events to generate new ideas and build participant commitment to self-initiated pilots without specifying exactly what will emerge from those activities. They play a critical role after pilots are launched through the way they support, embed and scale up successful pilot projects (Roehrig, Schwendenwein, & Bushe, 2015). Without committed and engaged sponsors providing leadership after events, even the most enlivening and generative events will have little sustained impact. We have witnessed this pattern of a lack of committed follow through from sponsors in generative change processes as a problem in organizations, but even more likely to be a problem in larger systems, ranging from inter-agency community service initiatives to the Paris Climate Accords.

Additionally, unlike organizations with more unified and established authority structures, societal problems that cross multiple boundaries involve a greater diversity of actors, and typically require competing jurisdictions, interest groups, governing bodies and even nation-states to put their differences aside and form a coalition of sponsors. Successful use of generative change methods at this level probably requires the initial formation of a sponsoring coalition that increases their active commitment and support as successful pilot results emerge. One successful example would be the UN Global Compact. As of 2019 this is the world's largest corporate social responsibility initiative with 13,000 corporate participants and other stakeholders in over 170 countries. UN Secretary-General Kofi Annan initiated this generative change process, supported by Professor and Dialogic OD consultant David Cooperrider, in July 2000. It brought together over 100 leaders of the largest multinational corporations to set the purpose and guidelines for what they named The Global Compact. While not in name, in practice they became the sponsoring coalition that has supported a two decade long journey that has produced thousands of pilot projects, many successful, worldwide (see www.unglobalcompact.org and https://aim-2flourish.com).

Conditions for convivial emergence

The Generative Change Model works with self-organizing processes to create change. However, self-organization does not necessarily assure that what emerges will promote the collective good as defined by the diverse stakeholders affected by the adaptive challenge. If we ask the question, "under what conditions will people collectively organize in service to the greater good" two things stand out.

One is a common purpose. This is normally what drives effective generative change processes in organizations. The early stages of the Generative Change Model rest crucially on sponsors' and change agents' ability to articulate a purpose that addresses the adaptive challenge and captures and sustains stakeholders' interest and energy. Global crises tend to be framed as problems to be fixed following mechanistic imagery, or an enemy to be vanquished, following wartime imagery. Framing crises in this way might temporarily mobilize enough actions to do away with an immediate threat but is less likely to energize committed actions to realize collectively agreed-upon purposes that advance the greater good.

Consider the implications when something like the Covid-19 pandemic is framed as a war. There will be enemies and allies, casualties, front-line troops, searches for weapons and strategies to defeat and eliminate the threat, and calls for militaristic command and control leaders to take charge and articulate the war plans for their theater of operations. What if responses to the pandemic were framed by an agreed-upon purpose like "health and resilience for all"? Such a framing invites globally coordinated actions where success, by definition, requires that all actors must realize positive benefits. It might also stimulate leadership and actions that promote sustained, positive, collaborative innovation in contrast to command-and-control actions to destroy or eliminate an immediate threat.

A different condition that supports convivial emergence is a common identity, a sense of "we" that bridges stakeholders' existing differences. Without a common purpose to bind together people who don't initially have a common identity, self-organizing processes tend to fragment into different initiatives, each furthering the needs and interests of separate stakeholders who do have a group identity. This state of fragmentation can exist in organizations and sometimes the first challenge of a generative change is to create a sense of common identity among diverse stakeholders (Bushe, 2002; Newman & Fitzgerald, 2001; Powley, Fry, Barrett, & Bright, 2004). But even without a common identity, a common purpose can be enough. Only after a common purpose or common identity exists, however, can emergent change approaches hope to produce changes that will be good for all. Consider how at this point in history, a kind of tribalism is ascendent. Prior movement toward a more planetary sense of identity in the face of common challenges has reversed, with increasing differentiation of identities that lead to go it alone or competing strategies and actions. Some examples are the USA's current political climate, Brexit, ethnic nationalism flaring in Eastern Europe, anti-Muslim policies in India and Myanmar, to name just a few.

A hopeful perspective on our current situation is provided by the social science research that suggests successive phases of integration and differentiation are common to various developmental processes (e.g., Greiner, 1998; Phinney, 2013; Piaget, 1972). For example, the current breaking down of order has been observed in previous industrial revolutions, and the current one is no exception. "Big history" (Spier, 2010) suggests that we are at a threshold that will require us to reinvent social and governmental organization at a new level of complexity. Perhaps we will naturally find a path from our current differentiation to greater integration of global identity. That, in turn, will more readily support the utilization of generative change processes to successfully address global issues, which we hope will lead to a virtuous cycle of increasing use of generative change and an increasing sense of collective humankind.

Conclusion

Generative change processes have emerged in organization development to enable leaders to manage complexity and adaptive challenges better. Generative change has also been used for societal and, in a few cases, global issues. The requirements for their successful use at the societal level, however, have not been as thoroughly investigated. At least two challenges that are easier to resolve at the organizational than societal level have to be worked out. One is sponsorship. How do we create the degree of sponsorship required to support generative change at a global level? The second is the need for some commonality in either purpose or identity that leads people to self-organize for the common good. When dealing with fragmented group identities, how can we create enough of a sense of common identity, or common purpose, to support the emergence of convivial solutions to collective problems?

References

Bushe, G. R. (2002). Meaning making in teams: Appreciative inquiry with preidentity and postidentity groups. In R. Fry, F. Barrett, J. Seiling, & D. Whitney (Eds.), *Appreciative inquiry and organizational transformation: Reports from the field* (pp. 39–63). Westport, CT: Quorum.

Bushe, G. R. (2020). *The dynamics of generative change.* BMI.

Bushe, G. R., & Kassam, A. (2005). When is appreciative inquiry transformational? A meta-case analysis. *Journal of Applied Behavioral Science, 41*(2), 161–181. doi:10.1177/0021886304270337

Bushe, G. R., & Marshak, R. J. (2016). The dialogic mindset: Leading emergent change in a complex world. *Organization Development Journal, 34*(1), 37–65.

Bushe, G. R., & Marshak, R. J. (Eds.). (2015a). *Dialogic Organization development: The theory and practice of transformational change.* Berrett-Koehler.

Bushe, G. R., & Marshak, R. J. (2015b). Introduction to the dialogic organization development mindset. In G. Bushe & R. Marshak (Eds.), *Dialogic organization development: The theory and practice of transformational change* (pp. 11–32). Berrett-Koehler.

Bushe, G. R. & Marshak, R. J. (2014). The dialogic mindset in organization development. *Research in Organizational Change and Development, 22*, 55–97. doi:10.1108/S0897-301620140000022002

Bushe, G. R., & Marshak, R. J. (2009). Revisioning organization development: Diagnostic and dialogic premises and patterns of practice. *The Journal of Applied Behavioral Science, 45*(3), 348–368. doi:10.1177/0021886309335070

Bushe, G. R., & Storch, J. (2015). Generative image: Sourcing novelty. In G. Bushe & R. Marshak (Eds.), *Dialogic organization development: The theory and practice of transformational change* (pp. 101–122). Berrett-Koehler.

Cooperrider, D. L. (2012). The concentration effect of strengths: How the whole system "AI" summit brings out the best in human enterprise. *Organization Dynamics, 41*, 106–117. dx.doi.org/10.1016/j.orgdyn.2012.01.004

Davies, A. (1992). Setting national and local priorities: Australian consumer forum for the aged. In M. Weisbord (Ed.), *Discovering common ground* (pp. 265–281). Berrett-Koehler.

Finegold, M. A., Holland, B. M., & Lingham, T. (2002). Appreciative inquiry and public dialogue: An approach to community change. *Public Organization Review*, *2*, 235–252. doi:10.1023/A:1020292413486

Greiner, L. E. (1998). Evolution and revolution as organizations grow, 1972. *Harvard Business Review*, *76*(3), 55–68.

Hastings, B. J., & Schwarz, G. M. (2019). Diagnostic and dialogic organization development: Competitive or collaborative focuses of inquiry? In *Academy of Management Proceedings* (Vol. *2019*, pp. 10662). Academy of Management, Briarcliff Manor.

Heifetz, R. A. (1998). *Leadership without easy answers*. Harvard University Press.

Huzzard, T., Hellström, A., & Lifvergren, S. (2014). System-wide change in cancer care: Exploring sensemaking, sensegiving, and consent. *Research in Organization Change and Development*, *22*, 191–218. doi:10.1108/S0897-301620140000022005

Lukensmeyer, C. J. (2015). *Bringing citizen voices to the table: A guide for public managers*. Jossey-Bass.

Marshak, R. J., & Bushe, G. R. (2018). Planned and generative change in organization development. *Organization Development Practitioner*, *50*(4), 9–15.

Mirabeau, L., & Maguire, S. (2014). From autonomous strategic behavior to emergent strategy. *Strategic Management Journal*, *35*(8), 1202–1229.

Newman, H. L., & Fitzgerald, S. P. (2001). Appreciative inquiry with an executive team: Moving along the action research continuum. *Organization Development Journal*, *19*(3), 37–43.

Phinney, J. S. (2013). Multiple group identities: Differentiation, conflict and integration. In J. Kroger (Ed.), *Discussions on ego identity* (pp. 47–74). Psychology Press.

Piaget, J. (1972). *The principles of genetic epistemology*. Basic Books.

Powley, E. H., Fry, R. E., Barrett, F. J., & Bright, D. S. (2004). Dialogic democracy meets command and control: Transformation through the appreciative inquiry summit. *Academy of Management Executive*, *18*(3), 67–80. doi:10.5465/AME.2004.14776170

Roehrig, M. J., Schwendenwein, J. & Bushe, G. R. (2015). Amplifying change: A three-phase approach to model, nurture, and embed ideas for change. In G. Bushe & R. Marshak (Eds.), *Dialogic Organization development: The theory and practice of transformational change* (325–348). Berrett-Koehler.

Rowland, D., & Higgs, M. (2008). *Sustaining change*. San Francisco: Jossey-Bass.

Schwass, G. (1992). A conservation strategy for Pakistan. In M. R. Weisbord (Ed.), *Discovering common ground* (pp. 159–169). Berrett-Koehler.

Snowden, D. J. (2002). Complex acts of knowing: Paradox and descriptive self awareness. *Special Issue of the Journal of Knowledge Management*, *6*(2), 1–27.

Spicer, A., & Hyatt, D. (2017). Walmart's emergent low-cost sustainable product strategy. *California Management Review*, *59*(2), 116 –141. doi:10.1177/0008125617695287

Spier, F. (2010). *Big history and the future of humanity*. Wiley-Blackwell.

5 When the stakes are high and trust is low

Colleen Magner and Adam Kahane

Reos Partners, https://reospartners.com/, works with complex social challenges, for example, advancing energy transitions in the US and South Africa, addressing structural racism with a large international NGO, and exploring alternative education futures in Brazil.

Our aim in all our work is to transform the social systems in which issues like these are embedded so that they function better for all those involved. We start with convening leaders across a system who are interested, influential and insightful about the issues being discussed, and who are connected to other efforts to address the issue. We carry out a number of structured activities including interviews, learning journeys and workshops in which we use methodologies that are systemic, collaborative and experimental, that engage and enable participants to slow down and step into uncertainty.

Sometimes, these processes include Transformative Scenario Planning, https://reospartners.com/tools/transformative-scenarios/, which are structured, creative processes in which diverse actors develop possible futures and strategic options related to a complex challenge, and Social Labs, https://reospartners.com/tools/social-labs/, which are intensive, experimental processes that bring together actors who are ready to act together in order to address that complex challenge. We have built and operated such platforms to address issues from child nutrition, https://reospartners.com/projects/bhavishya-alliance-for-child-nutrition/, to education, https://reospartners.com/projects/emergency-aid-lab/.

Our work builds on the approaches identified by others about what is necessary for systems change. For example, it is consistent with the principle developed by Weisbord and Janoff (2010) that for success to occur in change it is necessary to have the "whole system" gathered together. It is also consistent with the recognition by Bushe and Marshak (2015) and others that focuses on the importance of dialogue. It aligns with the importance that competitors collaborate with each other, especially during times of crisis (e.g. Amis & Janz, 2020, Teirney, 2011).

DOI: 10.4324/9781003109372-6

Our work has also built on these approaches, and evolved four concepts of what collaboration under such conditions requires. We describe each below. One is stretch collaboration, a concept Adam Kahane (2017) developed that extends beyond typical scholarly and practitioner approaches to collaboration. We briefly summarize each concept below. We include three components of stretch collaboration.

Needing to work with people we don't like or trust

One of the most important lessons we've learned is one we have all heard before: Different people have different stories. This is not a new idea, but we emphasize it because we keep encountering groups of people who are so committed to their own stories that they have trouble seeing anyone else's. Oil pipeline projects all over the world are a perfect illustration of this. In our experience of working on this issue, these projects are often difficult to execute because they are major infrastructure undertakings with large economic and environmental impacts and, as such, are visible symbols of the high-stakes conflicts around these issues. Such projects also illustrate a fundamental principle in addressing a challenge: Sustainable solutions to complex problems are rarely simple or linear. Just like pipelines, they must twist and turn (Kahane, 2018c).

With pipelines, there are many interests and stakes at play: Those who want pipelines to access new markets so more oil can be sold at higher prices and thereby increase revenues, royalties and employment; those who want to protect terrestrial and aquatic environments and tourism against disruption from oil spills and tanker traffic; indigenous and other communities along proposed pipeline routes who want their rights respected and to negotiate either to avoid negative impacts by the project or to achieve economic benefits from it; individuals and organizations concerned about climate change who want high-carbon fuel to remain in the ground; or governments who want to find ways to balance some or all of these objectives.

In contentious situations like this, there is no single paramount interest or best answer. And yet for stakeholders who are convinced that their way is the right way, this multiplicity of interests feels supremely frustrating and impossible to resolve. But it *is* possible to find a way forward in such situations. It requires that at least some of the players work earnestly to recognize the multiple interests at play. This is simple but not easy. We need to engage others with curiosity about their reality, frankness about your own, and a genuine willingness to change what you are thinking and doing.

The importance of hope

A question was once asked by one of the participants of a process we facilitated aimed at reducing violence against women: "Could we come at this issue from a different place?" In exploring ways to come at this issue from a different place, one of the younger activist participants spoke about the importance of collective movements of resistance; that going at this fight alone or in pockets of resistance was futile. In our experience, the "different place" is in part about sharing different perspectives of perceiving the issue and building relationships to act collaboratively. The process we facilitated with this group started with constituting about 40 people who work across government, civil society and the donor community. The second phase included creating multiple opportunities to share perspectives and experiences and allow for a bigger "system view" of the issue to emerge. From that picture, the group explored and tested where there might be innovative ideas to address the endemic problem of violence against women. This process took almost a year to get to this point – the point where we cannot underestimate hope as a catalyst for collaboration.

Our experience of hope isn't a fixed idea of what should happen. Hope is a vague but strong pull to believe that something could be different. As we started to see some clues for where there are opportunities that we might not have seen before, it's precisely in that hazy view that we could come at this work from a different place, which is an important moment to recognize in a process (Magner, 2018). When it is clear that the situation is unsustainable to all involved, this is when the vague emergence of a necessary and different approach translates into hope. In this example, we have been surrounded by many women who have been personally affected by violence. Their experiences can bring agency for a different future, and one that has created new alliances across traditionally very different perspectives. Collaboration doesn't mean that hope will prevail and get you what you want. The higher potential of collaboration with diverse others is that together you'll be able to understand more of your situation and so will be able to create new options that are better than the ones you'd been able to imagine or implement separately – better than forcing, adapting, or exiting (Kahane, 2018a). Sometimes we need to fight. Choosing to collaborate is a pragmatic choice, often when high levels of complexity exist, and where a clear way forward is not apparent.

Successful collaboration requires a "stretch"

What if the people in the room can't even agree on what the problem is, much less how to solve it? What if there is low trust among them and no one who can control the situation? What if the only thing people can agree on is that the situation is unacceptable and must be changed?

In this context, collaboration means something different from – and more difficult than – the standard interpretation. The typical definition of collaboration gives way to the secondary meaning: The fear that if you work with the enemy, you will be seen as a "collaborator", and even your allies will distrust you and maybe punish you (Kahane, 2018). When we asked President Juan Manuel Santos of Colombia, who won a Nobel Peace Prize for negotiating the peace treaty, what was most difficult for him in these processes he answered: "The hardest part was being considered a traitor". In these sorts of situations, the conventional approach to collaboration will not work. But the good news is *it doesn't have to*. You don't have to give up when people don't agree.

Often, the best timing for "stretch collaboration" is when there are high levels of frustration across different centers of power, and yet also a sense of what is possible (Magner, 2018). For example, at a training workshop in Jos, a city in northern Nigeria where we had been invited to train several senior government officials on scenario planning following national elections, a participant asked with frustration: "How can we change the mindset of people so that they move beyond the short-term, 'get what I can gain' mentality, to realizing that this country can only succeed with a collective, long-term view?" This question resonated with us as much as it did with the audience, who applauded and murmured in agreement. How can we look at a situation and extract new insight from it? Or even better, how can we collectively look at an issue and extract *a collaborative* insight from it?

In conventional terms, we assume that to successfully collaborate, we must strive for an agreement on what the problem is that we are trying to solve and share a common vision for how the problem should be addressed. The first "stretch" proposed is that collaboration requires both conflict and connection. Secondly, conventional collaboration focuses on identifying a solution as quickly as possible and creating a plan to achieve it. Stretch collaboration suggests that, when the future is highly volatile and contested, we need to experiment our way forward. Thirdly, conventional collaboration tries to advocate for influencing others' actions – to change "them". The third stretch suggests that we need to change ourselves and others, and step into the game.

Stretch 1: Creating safe spaces for conflict and connection

The collaborative act of embracing conflict and connection when power is unequal plays out frequently when we talk about race. In our work, addressing increasing inequality and its manifestations, our colleagues are often confronted with the dynamics of race, particularly in groups. How do we talk about and acknowledge the realities and perceptions about race and privilege? Without surfacing these dynamics in a group, the exercise will always be flawed, since the discussion will be based on the naïve assumption that the starting point is a level playing field.

Collaboration is not about transcending the past so that we see the world in the same way, but about the willingness to commit to addressing the issues and to staying in a relationship with one another, even when it seems to be the more difficult option. How then is a "safe space" created to have a conversation about such issues as race and inequality, within the context that we are trying to change? It requires us to acknowledge that people embody multiple roles at the same time – as a person, as a representative of an organization or as a member of a particular racial group trying to find a way through the compromised world that we live in. In the continuous pursuit of reinventing these relationships, conflict that arises from acknowledging power dynamics is sometimes inevitable and necessary. This is important to both acknowledge and understand in the group in order to create a safe space (Bojer, Roehl, Knuth, & Magner, 2008).

We have learned from the work of Myrna Lewis, called Deep Democracy, that the approach helps to surface and give expression to what is otherwise left unsaid, https://deep-democracy.net. A key aspect of Deep Democracy is that the process focuses on roles and relationships rather than on individuals. A role is usually held by more than one individual, and an individual usually holds more than one role in the group. The most personal is linked to the universal, in that each person actually has the capacity and potential to express any role. S/he has both an individual identity as well as access to the overall pattern and knowledge of the whole. A system will tend to be healthier if roles are fluid and shared. We've usually observed that this sort of shift in self-perception comes about through confrontations, challenges and feedback that's unsettling and shows us that we're not as we thought we were, as well as opportunities to share with people who are quite different from us. The learning required is how to be in both conflict *and* relationship in our different roles. It is not a choice between the two; it is the dual nature that is required of this work.

Stretch 2: Courageously experimenting our way forward

The Violence Against Women Social Lab in South Africa mentioned earlier was convened in 2015 by the Soul City Institute for Social Justice and brought together leaders from across government departments, non-profit organizations, social activist movements and donors. Many of the members identified that one of the main reasons that the endemic problems of violence against women exist in South Africa is because of the inability to collaborate across sectors to address the issue. But for many months, attempts to identify opportunities for collaboration in the social lab were unraveled by expressions of conflict and mistrust.

However, through allowing participants to express their frustration, despair and blame, we experienced connection which enabled a safer space for new insights to emerge – participants had "released" their tightly held views about what needed to happen. It was not an obvious moment but, once it happened, there was a different quality in the relationship between participants across sectors, and a number of collaborative initiatives were spawned. It was, however, prefaced by a series of stuck interactions that had previously created a lot of pain and confusion for the lab members as well as for the facilitation team. The process of failure is a natural part of creating a swing to an alternative.

Groups get unstuck only when they try something different and keep trying until they discover what works. As we help people try and imagine a new and often more efficient way of finding solutions, we address two inter-related questions: How do we help teams move from a fear-based response to a more creative and open response? And then, how do we move from one fixed view of an outcome towards experimenting with multiple ideas to come up with a new way of doing things?

The realm of radical imagination involves finding more creative ways to resolve stuck situations that are not working optimally. Hard evidence shows that creativity yields more effective outputs, and the birthplace of creativity is our collective imagination (Magner, 2020). Amis writes about innovation during the times of COVID-19, but that successful innovation requires the ability to harness collective insight of a group, and a willingness to engage rapidly with new ideas (Amis, & Janz, 2020). The primary impediment to such fluidity is the rigidity that arises from fear that if we admit, to others or even to ourselves, that what we're doing is wrong, we'll lose out. The antidote to unfamiliarity isn't fear. It's a curiosity to experiment. And curiosity only comes with a dose of courage. It's a good reminder to listen to Maya Angelou's wise words:

> Courage is the most important of all the virtues, because without courage you can't practice any other virtue consistently. You can practice any virtue erratically, but nothing consistently without courage.
>
> (Angelou, 2008)

Stretch 3: Recognizing your role in the game

In 1998 in a lakeside town in the highlands of Guatemala, Hugo Beteta, a foundation executive, and Otilia Lux de Coti, an indigenous human rights campaigner, went for a walk. They were an unlikely pair. The country had been mired in a genocidal civil war in which the Guatemalan army had murdered hundreds of thousands of indigenous people, and Hugo and Otilia came from two worlds that were almost completely separated, politically, socially and culturally. But in 1996, the government and the rebels had signed a peace treaty to end the war. On the day Hugo and Otilia took their walk, we were facilitating a leadership workshop on how to implement the peace accords and invited the participants to choose a partner who was most different from them and go for a 45-minute stroll outside the hotel (Kahane, 2020b).

Hugo explained what happened in his walk "Otilia told me a story about her high school graduation that really shook me up. She'd received the highest grades of any graduating student and was given the honor of carrying the national flag onto the stage, but the school wouldn't allow her to wear her traditional ethnic clothing to the ceremony. So, she was forced to choose between having her accomplishment recognized and offending her family and betraying herself", he said. "I hadn't grasped how we Guatemalans have built everyday mechanisms for perpetuating the racism and inequality that produced the genocide". This is the act of recognizing his role in the game. These shifts in perspective helped the group make progress. Over the years that followed, the participants took significant actions to recognize and shift their role, separately and together, to build a better future for their country, including greater indigenous inclusion. Hugo, by the way, became minister of finance, and Otilia was appointed minister of culture. The strongest spur to changing what you're doing is not so much seeing your situation differently as seeing *yourself* differently.

Imagine and move towards possible futures

On December 3, 2019, a remarkable event took place in a hotel ballroom in Addis Ababa, Ethiopia. Forty national leaders from every major political tendency, region, and ethnic and religious group stood on the stage – in front of national and international dignitaries and media, and broadcasting live to an even wider audience – and read a declaration of the actions they would take, together, to improve the country's future (Kahane, 2020a). The team members on stage named themselves the Destiny Ethiopia team, after a year-long process to develop scenarios about the future of the country.

For Ethiopians to transform their country democratically and sustainably – rather than forcibly and temporarily – they will need to build trust with one another.

At the conclusion of their second workshop, one team member, an opposition politician, was standing on the front steps of the hotel where they had been meeting. In the weeks prior to the event, during an upsurge of deadly political violence, members of his party had been rounded up by the government, and so he had been frightened about coming to the workshop and had asked the meeting organizer to arrange for him to travel, disguised, in a convoy guarded by commandos. On that last day of the second workshop, the organizer asked the politician if he needed the same arrangements made for his trip back to the capital. The politician gestured toward his government counterpart, who was standing nearby. "No", the politician said, "I'll ride back with him". This politician made this dramatic shift as a result of meeting with, observing, and talking with his opponents during the workshops. Such a process for building trust is not complicated but it is crucial.

The event in the Addis Ababa hotel, six months later made an impact on the country because it made visible the new symbols and metaphors, and trust that the team had built among themselves and, by doing so, gave other citizens hope that they could do the same and succeed in transforming their nation. A common theme in the testimonials at the launch was, "I thought that it would be impossible for us to work together, but I discovered that it is possible".

Using a similar approach, we facilitated a process in the Omasati Region of Northern Namibia on the ASSAR (Adaptation at Scale in Semi-Arid Regions) project aimed to build resilience in local communities to more effectively address potential future climate shocks (Magner, 2015). The times together were intense as the group spent long hours contemplating how to respond to these futures that might unfold. And yet, everyone remained in the year-long process. Despite disagreements, they were committed to prioritizing activities they could work on together in response to these likely futures.

An impact review among participants highlighted that they particularly appreciate the way in which the process builds a new capacity to imagine possible futures. Participants value how it better allows them to weave together a number of messy and complex variables than conventional strategy-methods allow for. Everyone involved indicated that there are no shortcuts in this process to strengthen trust, build long-term planning skills and more effectively adapt to climate change in local ways.

In conclusion, these stories about the future activate vastly different responses, none of which we would have predicted. The point of imagining possible futures together is to unlock our imagination to respond. And in those many activated responses, we transform the future.

Acknowledgments

We gratefully acknowledge our colleague Tshekgofatso Nkwane, who helped with the research for this chapter.

Reference list

Amis, J. M., & Janz, B. D. (2020). Leading change in response to COVID-19. *The Journal of Applied Behavioral Science, 56*(3), 272–278. Retrieved from https://journals.sagepub.com/doi/pdf/10.1177/0021886320936703

Angelou, M. (2008). Cornell Chronicle. Retrieved from https://news.cornell.edu/stories/2008/05/courage-most-important-virtue-maya-angelou-tells-seniors

Bojer, M., Roehl, H., Knuth, M., & Magner, C. (2008). *Mapping dialogue: Essential tools for social change.* Chagrin Falls, OH: Taos Institute. Retrieved from https://www.taosinstitute.net/product/mapping-dialogue-essential-tools-for-change-by-marianne-mille-bojer-heiko-roehl-marianne-knuth-and-colleen-magner

Bushe, G., & Marshak, R. (2015). *Dialogic Organization development: The theory and practice of transformational change.* Oakland, CA: Berrett-Koehler Publishers. Retrieved from https://www.amazon.com/Dialogic-Organization-Development-Practice-Transformational/dp/1626564043

Kahane, A. (2017). *Collaborating with the enemy: How to work with people you don't agree with or like or trust.* San Francisco, CA: Berrett-Koehler. Retrieved from https://www.bkconnection.com/books/title/Collaborating-with-the-Enemy

Kahane, A. (2018a). Collaborating isn't the only option. *Strategy & Business.* Retrieved from https://www.strategy-business.com/blog/Collaborating-Isnt-the-Only-Option?gko=e6734

Kahane, A. (2018b). How to collaborate when you don't have consensus. *Strategy & Business.* Retrieved from https://www.strategy-business.com/article/How-to-Collaborate-When-You-Dont-Have-Consensus?gko=cc3fe

Kahane, A. (2018c). Progress doesn't always follow a straight line. *Strategy & Business.* Retrieved from https://www.strategy-business.com/blog/Progress-Doesnt-Always-Follow-a-Straight-Line?gko=06f34

Kahane, A. (2020a). Transformation requires trust. *Strategy & Business.* https://www.strategy-business.com/blog/Transformation-requires-trust?gko=cf1a9

Kahane, A. (2020b). Walk your way to transformation. *Strategy & Business.* https://www.strategy-business.com/blog/Walk-your-way-to-transformation?gko=90b57

Magner, C. (2015). Does it have to be so difficult? Moving through tough terrain series. Retrieved from https://reospartners.com/does-it-have-to-be-so-difficult/

Magner, C. (2018). What kind of collaboration do we need to take South Africa forward? *Trialogue Business in Society Handbook.* Retrieved from https://reospartners.com/publications/what-kind-of-collaboration-is-needed-to-move-south-africa-forward/

Magner, C. (2020). Facing down crisis with radical imagination and experimentation. *GIBS Acumen Magazine.* Issue 33. Third Quarter. Retrieved from https://mags.contactmedia.co.za/acumen/33/

Weisbord, M., & Janoff, S. (2010). *Future search: Getting the whole system in the room for vision, commitment and action* (3rd ed.). Oakland, CA: Berrett-Koehler. Retrieved from https://www.bkconnection.com/books/title/future-search

Part II

Attention to political, national, and cross-national systems

6 Should capitalism be reimagined?

If so, how?

Rebecca Henderson

Capitalism is one of the great inventions of the human race: an unparalleled engine of prosperity, innovation, and individual freedom that has lifted billions of people out of poverty. But its very success has contributed to levels of inequality not seen since the 1920s. In the US and the UK those at the bottom of the income distribution have not had a significant pay raise in the last 20 years. Social mobility has fallen dramatically, while across the world racial and ethnic minorities continue to be largely excluded from the economic mainstream.

Capitalism's success is also driving massive environmental degradation. Left unchecked, global warming promises to destabilize the climate, threaten the world's food supply, flood many of the great coastal cities and force millions of people to migrate. Plastic chokes the world's oceans. One million of the world's eight million species are threatened with extinction, while the burning of fossil fuels continues to cause enormous damage to human health every year. Emissions have fallen (slightly) in the face of the COVID-19 pandemic but they are poised to bounce back hard and fast (International Energy Agency, 2021).

What happened?

The problems we face have many causes, but one of them is that we have allowed our societies to get radically out of balance. As a long literature in political science and development economics has suggested, healthy, inclusive societies rest on three foundations: A free market; a strong civil society; and a democratically elected, transparent, capable and responsive government. Together these three institutions hold each other accountable, balancing the power of the free market with the need to provide public goods and the need to ensure that the market remains both free and fair (Acemoglu & Robinson, 2012).

In the US, in the 1960s and 1970s, this balance was broadly understood. Businesses saw themselves as partners in generating prosperity

DOI: 10.4324/9781003109372-8

The First Best Solution:
Rebuilding Inclusive Institutions

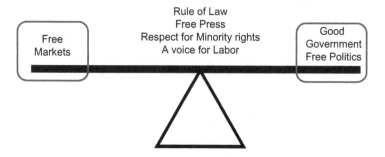

Figure 6.1 The three pillars of a strong society

that benefited everyone. But by the early 1980s, managers in much of the developed world had begun to believe that their sole responsibility was to increase profits, even if that meant dumping greenhouse gases into the atmosphere, driving down wages so low that employees were forced to depend on government support and lobbying for rules and regulations that favored only themselves.

This belief in profits alone arose from a transformation in economic thinking pioneered by Milton Friedman and his colleagues at the University of Chicago following World War II that suggested that to do anything other than maximize profits – to charge less than the market will bear for a life-saving drug for example – was not only to abandon your duties as your investors' agent but also to make society poorer and less free (Mirowski & Deiter Piehwe, 2009).

But as the economy has flourished, the world around it has not. It has become increasingly clear that markets require adult supervision – that they only lead to prosperity and freedom when they are genuinely free and fair. Intuitively, if firms can dump toxic waste into rivers, lie to their consumers, and form alliances to fix prices, there is no guarantee that maximizing profits will increase either aggregate wealth or individual freedom.

In short, global capitalism looks less and less like the textbook model of free and fair markets enabled and controlled by civil society and democratic government on which the injunction to focus solely on profit maximization was based. It's not surprising, then, that we are increasingly neither prosperous nor free. Left unchecked, markets are subject to powerful incentives to destroy the natural and social worlds around them.

Maximizing shareholder value is therefore no longer likely to maximize either prosperity or freedom. If these remain the fundamental normative commitments of capitalism, the first step towards reimagining capitalism is to embrace the idea that firms also have a duty to support the health of the natural, social and institutional systems in which they are embedded.

The good news is that business has a compelling economic case for action. It will be much easier to make money in a world in which the climate is relatively stable, in which the major coastal cities are not under water and in which agricultural collapse is not routinely triggering the migration of hostile, hungry populations (IPCC, 2014). Moreover, the private sector will benefit from a world that has significantly less poverty and inequality (Buckman et al., 2021).

But this is a collective case, and it might therefore seem unlikely that any but the most visionary and confident business leaders would attempt to act on it. What, then, can be done?

The current move towards shared value, or towards the simultaneous creation of private profit and public benefit is a critical first step. The evidence that there are broad opportunities to create shared value is extensive. Walmart saved about $1bn a year by redesigning its trucking fleet to reduce energy use. Tesla has become one of the most valuable automakers in the world. Firms that adopt high road employment strategies – that is, that create jobs that pay well, treat employees with dignity and respect and grant them significant discretion to shape their own work and build a collective sense of purpose – have repeatedly found that the strategy creates significant economic value (Henderson, 2020a, 2021).

Although such actions are sometimes derided as greenwashing or dismissed as too small or local to have any real impact, they often drive broader change. They act as demonstration projects: Proving that a private business can solve a public problem, driving down the costs of new technologies and demonstrating that new business models are indeed feasible. Tesla's embrace of electrically powered vehicles, for example, probably accelerated the transformation of the automotive industry by at least five years. Walmart's embrace of highly concentrated liquid detergents pushed the entire industry into moving in the same direction.

As a second step, firms can drive change through coordinated action. While there are many opportunities for firms to make money and address social or environmental problems at the same time, there are also many that can only be exploited if firms act together. The move to preserve the world's fisheries is a prime example (Henderson, 2016). While every firm will benefit if everyone reduces their catch, no single firm can profit from doing so alone. Since many fishers understand these dynamics, roughly half the world's fisheries are now sustainably fished. Similar logic has led to the emergence of cooperative arrangements to tackle the twin problems of sustainability and unacceptable labor practices in cocoa, palm oil, beef, textiles, and mining and minerals. For example, a group of consumer goods companies seeking to reduce deforestation in order to protect their brands was able to persuade the buyers of more than 60% of the world's publicly traded palm oil to join them in a commitment to buy only sustainable grown oil.

In some cases, these voluntary self-regulatory arrangements have been extremely successful. Cooperative arrangements significantly reduced deforestation in the Brazilian Amazon for many years. But they are often unstable. Without any real penalty for failing to cooperate, firms are often tempted to renege on their commitments and revert to business as usual.

Who – or what – might be capable of policing cooperation between firms, essentially forcing them all to do the right thing and leaving no one at a competitive disadvantage if they do? There are two possibilities. The first is investors. A very large fraction of the world's financial assets is controlled by roughly 12 firms. These firms are so large that they cannot diversify away from the threat of catastrophic risks such as climate change (Henderson, 2020b). Some of the world's wealthiest owners are similarly exposed. The Japanese government pension fund, for example, is worth more than $1.6 trillion and owns roughly 1% of the world's equity markets. Hiro Mizuno, who was its chief investment officer until early 2020, came to believe that solving problems like social inclusion and climate change was central to his fiduciary duty because they posed severe risks to his long-term returns (Henderson, Lerner, Serafeim, & Jinjo, 2020).

The emergence of ESG metrics (Environmental, Social and Governance) could give investors the means to insist that firms tackle environmental and social problems, and to track their performance as they do. More and more, investors are working together to push the firms they own to address both social and environmental risks. For example, more than 450 investors, representing $40 trillion in assets, have banded together to form Climate Action 100+, a group devoted to pushing the world's 100 largest emitters to set concrete targets for reducing carbon emissions and transitioning to a carbon free economy.

The second institution that might force firms to do the right thing is, of course, government. If governments worldwide regulated or priced carbon emissions, for example, it would be in every firm's economic interest to solve climate change (Cramton, 2017). If governments strengthened labor regulations, making it illegal to pay any worker less than a living wage, if they invested heavily in education and health, actively supported employee organization and aggressively taxed the wealthy, inequality would fall. If it were illegal for corporations to flood the political system with money and if anti-trust regulations were routinely enforced, the largest and most powerful firms would be much less able to shape the rules of the game in their own favor (Zingales, 2013).

Could business actually help to rebuild our institutions? Possibly. Businesspeople are already coming together to lobby in favor of carbon regulation and against money in politics. We Are Still In, for example, brings more than 2,000 firms together with NGOs, faith communities, and city and state governments to lobby for pollution reduction targets which will allow the US to comply with the Paris climate agreement. The NGOs American Promise and Leadership Now coordinate networks of business leaders committed to improving American democracy.

In the current environment it may be difficult to imagine the business community lobbying for the wholesale rebuilding of the institutions of an inclusive society, but it has happened before. Germany's private sector played an important role in developing Germany's current institutions, working collaboratively with organized labor to develop a system of apprenticeship training that is often cited as one of the central determinants of the country's low inequality and high productivity, and similar efforts played out in countries as diverse as Denmark and Mauritius (Henderson, 2020a).

Could it happen again? Could the private sector play a central role in rebuilding our democracies? Should it? It might seem an unlikely idea. But ask yourself – what is the alternative? If business stays silent, focused on profit alone, what will happen? The private sector must seize the chance to reimagine capitalism.

References

(All websites accessed February 8, 2021)

Acemoglu, D., & Robinson, J. A. (2012). *Why nations fail: The origins of power, prosperity and poverty*. New York: Crown Books.

Buckman, S. et al. (2021). The Economic Gains from Equity. Working Paper, San Francisco Federal Research, January 19, 2021. Retrieved from https://www.frbsf .org/our-district/files/economic-gains-from-equity.pdf

Cramton, P., Mackay, D., Ockenfels, A., & Stoft, S. (2017). *Global carbon pricing*. Cambridge, MA: MIT Press.

Henderson, R. (2016). *Note: Industry self-regulation: Sustaining the commons in the 21st century*. Harvard Business School Publishing, Note 9-315-074, March 2016.

Henderson, R. (2020a). *Reimagining capitalism in a world on fire*. New York: Public Affairs.

Henderson, R. (2020b). The unlikely environmentalists. *Foreign Affairs*. Retrieved from   https://www.foreignaffairs.com/articles/world/2020-04-13/unlikely -environmentalists

Henderson, R. (Forthcoming 2021). Tackling the big problems: Management science, innovation and purpose. *Management Science*. Retrieved from https:// pubsonline.informs.org/doi/10.1287/mnsc.2020.3746

Henderson, R., Lerner, J., Serafeim, G., & Jinjo, N. (2020). Can a pension fund change the world? Inside the GPIF's embrace of ESG. HBS case 9-319-067. February 2020.

International Energy Outlook 2020. Retrieved from https://www.iea.org/reports/ world-energy-outlook-2020

The International Energy Agency: "Global Energy Review 2021", April 2021. Available at: https://www.iea.org/reports/global-energy-review-2021. Accessed October 24, 2021.

The IPCC 5th Annual Assessment report, 2014. Retrieved from https://www.ipcc .ch/report/ar5/syr/

Mirowski, P., & Piehwe, D. (2009). *The road from Mont Pelerin: The making of the neoliberal thought collective*. Cambridge, MA: Harvard University Press.

Zingales, L. (2013). *Saving capitalism from the capitalists*. New York, NY: Harper Collins.

7 Pathway to balance

Henry Mintzberg

Communism, capitalism and populism are three ways to take a country out of balance, in favor, respectively, of their public sector governments, private sector businesses and certain plural sector communities (Mintzberg, 2015).

Few countries remain communist. In 1989, many of those regimes in Eastern Europe collapsed under the dead weight of their own imbalance. In contrast, at the time, most of the democracies of the West maintained a relative balance across the three sectors. But the mistaken belief that it was capitalism that had triumphed – brought down communism – has enabled exactly this to happen in many of these countries ever since.

The United States has led many of the "liberal democracies" toward a dangerous imbalance in favor of private sector interests. And this has, in turn, given rise to the countervailing power of narrow populist interests that have seized power in recent years, whether religious (as in Turkey), class (as in Venezuela) or nationalist (as in Hungary).

Accordingly, few countries today maintain relative balance, and most of these are small – for example, Denmark, New Zealand and Switzerland. Indeed, countries with less than about ten million people comprise 14 of the 22 countries listed as "Full Democracies" on the *Economist*'s 2019 Democracy Index.[1] With so much imbalance in the world today, especially in all three of the established superpowers, major problems continue to fester, globally and locally. These include income disparities, the spread of corruption in government and business, climate change and widespread anger and angst amidst many populations.

A number of easy fixes are being promoted to deal with the imbalance. None are working. Heroic leadership at the "top" is one: Find the person who will resolve the problems, only to discover that so much heroic leadership turns out to be autocratic or impotent. Formidable government planning is another: We have the nonsense of officials elected to four-year terms making decades-long plans to deal with climate change. Perhaps most popular, especially in the failing liberal democracies, are proposals to fix capitalism, what

DOI: 10.4324/9781003109372-9

can be called adjectival capitalism: Progressive Capitalism, Breakthrough Capitalism, Caring Capitalism, Conscious Capitalism, Inclusive Capitalism, Regenerative Capitalism, Sustainable Capitalism, Humanistic Capitalism and, most curious of all, Democratic Capitalism (capitalism being the noun, democracy the adjective).[2] Fixing capitalism will no more fix our broken societies than would fixing communism have fixed the broken societies of Eastern Europe. It is our societies that need fixing, by acting now to restore their balance. A pathway to restore balance is illustrated in Figure 7.1, leading from rejuvenation to reformation. We now have more social initiatives and social movements for constructive change than probably ever before in human history (Block, 2008), most of them in what I call the *plural sector*. It is just that their efforts are scattered, while the forces for self-interest work in concert. For the cause of balance, plural sector associations will have to get their collective act together.

What is this plural sector? It comprises a wide variety of mostly community associations, owned neither by the state nor by private investors. Some, called cooperatives, are owned by their members, others are owned by no-one, as in many trusts, hospitals, universities and NGOs, as well as the social initiatives and social movements mentioned above.

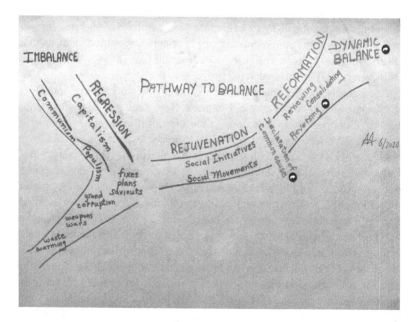

Figure 7.1 Pathway to balance

The sector is vast, yet obscure, having been lost in the century-old debate between left and right, public and private. Calling it *plural*, instead of the usual confusing mixture of inadequate labels (not-for-profit sector, third sector, civil society, etc.) can help it take its place alongside the sectors called *public* and *private*, especially to drive the kind of social change that we require.

When Franklin Delano Roosevelt, as President of the United States, was asked by an activist to support a social change, he replied: "I agree with you, now go out and make me do it". It is community groups in the plural sector, acting in concert, that make the authorities do it. These days, people can join together locally, in community groups networked globally, to challenge discredited authority, and offer more balanced alternatives in its place.

Interestingly enough, the most appropriate model for the change we require now may be that which occurred in 16th-century Europe. In 1517, an obscure monk named Martin Luther posted on the door of a church a one-page statement that challenged the corruption of the prevailing religion. This went quite literally viral within weeks, thanks to the new social medium of the time – the printing press: Luther's students carried the message to surrounding towns. What we now call the Reformation thus began from the ground up.[3] Today, likewise, a compelling statement of common cause could be the spark that begins the reformation we require. A group of us has developed a "Declaration of Our Interdependence" (2020) to suggest what form such a statement could take.[4]

Can some equivalent to reformation happen now, on a global scale? The deterioration of our climate is happening now, on that scale, as is rampant corruption, private and public, legal and criminal. Democracy is deteriorating now, far and wide, putting many people at risk from tyrants, and everyone at risk from nuclear weapons under the control of loose cannons. We have no choice but to engage in reformative change now.

We face an unprecedented puzzle, one that has no pat pieces that fit together neatly, nor does it come in a box with a cover that shows the vision to be constructed.[5] Pat solutions, however common, do not work for unprecedented puzzles. We have to create the pieces in the first place and then learn how to fit them together, one by one, to make an image that we have not seen before. In other words, we have to learn our way to a new vision, for a world where individual, communal and collective needs function in a dynamic balance, a world where universal collaboration will trump global devastation.

After I published *Rebalancing Society* in 2015, readers came back with one question above all: "What can I do?" I began a search for possible answers, and discovered there are so many, alongside some I added myself, that I drew them into a table,[6] according to what can be done personally, together in our communities, in our businesses, in our governments and altogether.

The plural sector is not "them". It is *you*, and *me*, and especially *we*, acting in concert – not as human resources serving the imbalance, but as resourceful human beings in the service of our progeny and our planet.

Notes

1 "Democracy Index 2019: A year of democratic setbacks and popular protest". A report by *The Economist* Intelligence Unit. The Economist Intelligence Unit Limited, 2020. www.eiu.com/topic/democracy-index.
2 "Getting past the adjectival capitalism fix, https://mintzberg.org/blog/getting -past-adjectival-capitalism-fix.
3 "Consolidation for Reformation", https://mintzberg.org/blog/consolidation-for -reformation.
4 https://ourinterdependence.org/.
5 "Going public with my puzzle", https://mintzberg.org/blog/going-public-with -my-puzzle.
6 A table of activities for rebalancing. https://ourinterdependence.org/table-of -activities/.

References

Block, P. (2008). *Community: The structure of belonging*. San Francisco, CA: Berrett-Koehler.
Declaration of Our Interdependence. (2020). *The Declaration of Our Interdependence*. Retrieved from https://ourinterdependence.org/
Mintzberg, H. (2015). *Rebalancing society: Radical renewal beyond left, right, and center*. Oakland, CA: Berrett-Koehler Publishers.

8 Gathering on the bridge

Co-creating our emerging equity-centered future

Yabome Gilpin-Jackson

Justice.
Equity.
Diversity.
Inclusion.

The COVID-19 pandemic has brought into popular discourse and lexicon the words above and many others that point to calls for social justice and the structural changes required of our world systems. To some, it has all been new. To others, who have been connected to and working in the critical social sciences, race, gender, identity and sexuality studies, or any social justice and change spaces fueled by the interdisciplinary and transdisciplinary social sciences, it is everyday language, research and experience. We, humanity, and the organizations and social systems we have designed, are at the center of the various global crises we face. Solving any of the challenges of our era fundamentally starts with addressing the inequities in our world that are at the roots of the crises we face, including inequities that have to date been kept firmly in place by a two-tiered global world system (Wallerstein, 2004). There is a Privileged system, which Wallerstein (2004) characterized in world-systems theory as made up of core countries; and a Marginalized system made up of peripheral countries. Core countries in world-systems theory are economically dominant and the holders of systemic power and hegemony, considered to have strong social, economic and political structures and labeled "developed" nations. Peripheral countries are the economically dependent countries, who supply labor to the privileged core and are overall considered to have weak social, economic and political structures and labeled "underdeveloped". While Wallerstein also distinguishes semi-peripheral countries, they are defined only by their pull towards becoming aligned with the core, so I focus here only on the Privileged and Marginalized systems.

DOI: 10.4324/9781003109372-10

We know that countries making up the Privileged system account for the dangerous levels of carbon emissions we face (Bressler, 2021). We know that Western knowledge systems dominated the world with colonization and devalued indigenous and other ways of knowing, being and governing (Prasad, Mills, Helms Mills, & Prasad, 2015). We know that the third and fourth industrial revolutions have created significant paradigm shifts and advanced our human systems but have also exacerbated global inequities (Schwab, 2016). We know from our collective lived experience of the COVID-19 pandemic that social inequalities, systemic racism and discrimination are mirrored across all aspects of society. We know that the majority of people categorized as frontline or essential workers serving society on the frontlines of the COVID-19 pandemic could not work from home and are disproportionately less educated and minority workers (Blau, Koebe, & Meyerhofer, 2020). We witnessed those who were disproportionately impacted in infection and death tolls; those who had access to vaccines and those who did not; those most economically impacted and those who continued to benefit; and in the midst, those subjected to continued police violence and institutional oppression and those who are not. And we have watched a groundswell of momentum towards calls for anti-racism and anti-oppression of all forms in our organizations and social systems buoyed by those who were already working on these issues – a call to the world for new equitable systems that recreate a world that works for all.

Over the past few months in my roles as executive leader, university instructor, consultant speaker and Board Chair of the Organization Development Network, I have delivered talks on these issues, sat on panels, facilitated conversations, co-edited a special journal issue (Bennett & Gilpin-Jackson, 2021) and coached and supported other leaders to think about the implications of centering justice, equity, diversity and inclusion in our organizations and in communities and what transformational change will require of us. A recurring theme of questions that surface in these conversations, is *How?*

How do we make the changes required of us?
How do we move past the overwhelm and crippling emotions to take action?
How do we include the marginalized without alienating the privileged?
How do we bridge the divides?

My starting point in response, is and will always be as Peter Block has written, that the answer to How is Yes (Block, 2003). Block writes:

> A major obstacle to acting on what matters is asking questions of methodology too quickly. I have symbolized this by obsessively focusing

on the question How? It's not that our pragmatic How? questions are not valid. It's just that when they define the debate we are deflected from considering our deeper values – plus asking How? is our favorite defense against taking action ... The alternative to asking How? Is saying Yes – not literally, but as a symbol of our stance towards the possibility of more meaningful change.

(Block, 2003, pp. 11, 27)

I believe we are at a threshold which we must push through to get to our transformations. The only way through, using a biblical journey narrative, is to embark on the journey from the Red Sea to the River Jordan, to get to our promised land. It may not be a straight path and will take us a metaphorical 40 years, but it will be worth it to overturn the 400 to thousands of years it took us to get here.

I have begun to formulate a way of thinking about navigating the complexity of this work that I call The Bridge Framework. This title is inspired by the often-quoted words from Nelson Mandela's 1994 inauguration speech: *The time for the healing of the wounds has come. The moment to bridge the chasms that divide us has come. The time to build is upon us* (South African Government News Agency, 2018). It applies specifically in contexts where historical inequities persist and there is a will to work towards transformation. It is an application of my "Grey Zone Change" thinking to justice, equity, diversity and inclusion work. Grey Zone Change is the space between the current state and the emerging future that is undefined and unknowable (Gilpin-Jackson, 2020a). In the grey zone, we accept that there are many questions and no simple answers, and we navigate it by intentionally doing the tough work needed to transition, learn and develop together to the emerging future, focused on possibility and courage. I envision, in the Bridge Framework, that the emerging future is metaphorically at the Gathering Place at the center of the bridge.

The Bridge Framework includes:

1. A Privileged system
   - The dominant core at every level of human systems within which many are concerned about global inequities and show up as conscious contributors to a decolonized and anti-oppressive way forward. However, there are also conscious and unconscious dynamics at play to maintain the privileges of being part of this system, leading to applications of power and political strategies to maintain the status quo. The struggle of people in the Privileged system who want to make a difference is overcoming blind spots and the feelings of guilt, shame or defensiveness to learn how to

engage differently, share power and actively use that same power to open access for others. An older White Male colleague said to me in a systemic change workshop on Power and Privilege, including anti-racism: "I feel powerless in these conversations. I don't have a voice because I don't get it. I feel stripped of my status and I don't know what to do to make a difference".

2. A Marginalized system

- The Marginalized periphery at every level of human systems is systematically forced to serve and support the Privileged system and bear the brunt of inequities that result from oppressive systems and structures. There is a conscious push for social justice and structural change to create a just and equitable world. Yet there are conscious, and unconscious pulls away to differentiation and alternative systems for reasons that range from survival to resistance. The struggle of those in Marginalized systems is learning to rebound from ongoing injustices and find sources of personal and psychological power to claim equality, rather than succumb to a vicious cycle of oppression. A Black Woman colleague said to me in the same workshop mentioned above, "I am tired of listening to the Privileged voices. They don't seem to understand how to truly listen and hear our voices too. All I've heard all my life is their side and their story. It's hard to feel hopeful for change when we can't achieve equilibrium of voices even in spaces like this".

3. Bridge Work

- Bridge Work represents pathways for the polarized Privileged and Marginalized systems to *join* instead of continue to *judge* each other from afar. This is the place where a shift in stance to the collaborative mindset required for systemic change and reminiscent of the mutual learning model is actualized (Argyris, 2005; Katz & Miller, 2021). Summarizing literature from Organization Development scholars and practitioners working at the intersection of systemic social change such as work chronicled in the NTL Handbook (Jones & Brazzel, 2014), the work that bridges Privileged and Marginalized systems can be categorized as:

  1. Systemic changes in the Hardware of Organizations – any work dealing with the systemic changes required in the infrastructure of organizations that centers equity in organization structures/design, internal systems such as policies, procedures, reward systems, technologies etc.

  2. Systemic changes in the Software of Organizations – anything dealing with the required shifts to cultural dynamics, leadership and the overall people experience to achieve justice and equity within systems.

3. Attention to Trauma-informed development. This calls for the need to acknowledge the impacts of systems of oppression for the purpose of processing trauma, achieving justice and accomplishing healing, without which there can be no progress towards systemic change and transformation. This is particularly important because addressing trauma is often part of the unconscious elements of group life. My research (Gilpin-Jackson, 2020b) has shown, however, that working through trauma at every level of human systems can lead to resonance, moments of awakening evoked from personal or collective narratives, that open space for transformation.

4. Meaningful contact between the Privileged and Marginalized systems. Collaborative change methodologies (Cady, 2019) are grounded in developing increased meaning-making and deeper consciousness at every level to move us to wholeness. We are emphasizing the power of the circle, small group, dialogue that evokes generativity and emergence, deliberation over debate and organizational and systemic learning. All this ultimately points to the need for contact in the gestalt sense of an exchange of energy across a boundary in which mutual influence and therefore the possibility for change occurs (Carter, 2019), which starts at the most basic interactional level with relational intelligence (Gilpin-Jackson, 2018).

5. Edgewalkers – these are the change agents and leaders working internally or from the outside-in to affect change and doing Bridge Work between the Privileged and Marginalized systems. I also use the term Edgewalkers to evoke the use of marginality as a site of resistance and possibility for those from Marginalized systems in working towards wholeness and liberation from the outside-in (hooks, 2015). It evokes the need for those from the Marginalized system to have access to the Privileged system, not just as tokens of inclusivity but with full access and permission to be centered in and directly influence the Bridge Work required to change the hardware and software of organizations and systems because "the edge is a space that enables bridges to be built and new stories to be told. In a world of emic perspectives, the challenge is to walk and work the edge" (Beals, Kidman, & Funaki, 2019, p. 600). It also invokes the need for those from Privileged systems to continually understand and leverage their social power in ways that best serve Bridge Work. It is the authentic allyship required to continue working towards the systemic changes

and transformations under way including when it requires decentering the Privileged self in service to the whole.

The material I have presented above suggests several implications and questions for thought and practice on the part of those wishing to build bridges in the midst of our global crises. I invite you to reflect on these three:

1. The world continues to work in the parallel systems of the Privileged and the Marginalized, even as all espouse working towards wholeness. For example, even as we in the social sciences are working to help people see systems and are developing a myriad of collaborative change methods as articulated in this book to shift the hardware and software of organizations and our world, I wonder whether we are having the intended impact. Who continues to be the majority voice in our collaborative processes? Do we have enough Edgewalkers to achieve meaningful contact across the divide of the Privileged and Marginalized systems? Ironically, the social sciences field overall is in the position of marginality and this book is an act of resistance and possibility to influence the Privileged system dominating the discourse of systemic change in our global crises.

2. We need acceptance of diverse Edgewalkers at scale from both the Privileged and Marginalized systems to achieve a tipping point to systemic change and transformation. Edgewalking presents a heavy toll on those that choose to engage in systemic change efforts especially when enacted as a solitary hero's journey. It can include the traumatic impacts of handling power holders, constant processing of trauma or re-traumatization and internalized or embodied impacts. When a critical mass of change agents is not present and supported, the Privileged system vilifies and works to eject Edgewalkers. On the other hand, the Marginalized system hails and idolizes those from the Privileged system who immerse themselves in the margins, due to internalized oppressive mindsets, thus perfectly replicating conditions of oppressive systems. Significant Bridge Work must be done to support communities of Edgewalkers for the journey to mitigate these likely impacts or address them in ways that heal (Frost & Robinson, 1999; Owusu & Wilde, 2021; Vivian, 2021). There is awareness of this and work underway in communities I am a part of, and I believe this work must be done to scale within as well as across systems.

3. If we take seriously the urgent need for Bridge Work to address our global crises, and understand that the time is NOW, what will it take to shift local and global communities from HOW to YES and to asking

questions such as: What Bridge Work must we embark on and what courage is required of us for the journey? What commitments are we willing to make and act on?

As a Black, African woman, with roots in Sierra Leone and Canada, from a lineage of Indigenous African Edgewalkers, who is married to a descendant of the freed and repatriated Black slaves to Africa and is a scholar–practitioner in these social sciences, my hope for the future is that I will live to see our world achieve system wholeness at the Gathering Place on the Bridge, healing our fault lines and co-creating a global equity-centered future for the next generation.

References

Argyris, C. (2005). Double-loop learning in organizations: A theory of action perspective. In K. G. Smith & M. A. Hitt (Eds.), *Great minds in management*. Oxford: Oxford University Press.

Beals, F., Kidman, J., & Funaki, H. (2019). Insider and outsider research: Negotiating self at the edge of the emic/etic divide. *Qualitative Inquiry*, *26*(6), 593–601. doi:10.1177/1077800419843950

Bennett, J. L., & Gilpin-Jackson, Y. (2021). Justice, equity, diversity & inclusion in organization development. *Organization Development Review: Special Issue*, *5*(3), 82.

Blau, F. D. B., Koebe, J., & Meyerhofer, P. A. (2020). Essential and frontline workers in the COVID-19 crisis. Retrieved from https://econofact.org/essential -and-frontline-workers-in-the-covid-19-crisis. Accessed on August 17.

Block, P. (2003). *The answer to how is yes: Acting on what matters*. San Francisco: Berrett-Koehler.

Bressler, R. D. (2021). The mortality cost of carbon. *Nature Communications*, *12*(1), 4467. doi:10.1038/s41467-021-24487-w

Cady, S. H. (2019). Collaborative change: Generative approaches that transform organizations, revitalize communities, and develop human potential. *Organization Development Review*, *51*(2), 21–25.

Carter, J., & GestaltOSD Center (2019). *Making a difference with your presence: Use of self and self-mastery*. Aitkin, MN: River Place Press.

Frost, P., & Robinson, S. (1999). The toxic handler: Organizational hero and casualty. *Harvard Business Review*, *77*(4), 96.

Gilpin-Jackson, Y. (2018). Where are you from? Building relational intelligence across identity differences. *Practising Social Change: A Journal of The NTL Institute of Applied Behavioural Sciences*.

Gilpin-Jackson, Y. (2020a). *Living, leading and facilitating in grey zone change*. Columbia, SC: Creative Commons/SLD Consulting.

Gilpin-Jackson, Y. (2020b). *Transformation after trauma: The power of resonance*. New York: Peter Lang Publishers.

hooks, b. (2015). *Feminist theory: From margin to center*. New York: Routledge.

Jones, B. B., & Brazzel, M. (2014). *The NTL handbook of organization development and change: Principles, practices, and perspectives*. Somerset: Center for Creative Leadership.

Katz, J. H., & Miller, F. A. (2021). Raising the bar on addressing inclusion, diversity and systemic change. *Organization Development Review*, *53*(3), 8–17.

Owusu, S. J., & Wilde, J. (2021). Transformative narrative technology and identities: Unknotting the heroic myth in organisation development. *Organization Development Review*, *53*(3), 65–72.

Prasad, A. (2015). Toward decolonizing modern Western structures of knowledge: A postcolonial interrogation of (Critical) Management Studies. In A. Prasad, P. Prasad, A. J. Mills & J. H. Mills (Eds.), *The Routledge Companion to Critical Management Studies* (pp. 185–223). London: Routledge. doi:10.4324/978131 5889818-21

Schwab, K. (2016). *The fourth industrial revolution*. World Economic Forum, New York: Crown Business.

South African Government News Agency (2018, May 10). Read: Nelson Mandela's inauguration speech as President of SA. Retrieved from https://www.sanews.gov.za/south-africa/read-nelson-mandelas-inauguration-za-inauguration-speech-president-sa

Vivian, P. (2021). Consultant as healer. *Organization Development Review*, *53*(3), 73–81.

Wallerstein, I. (2004). *World-system analysis: An introduction*. Durham, NC: Duke University Press.

9 Expanding relational coordination to tackle global crises

The Relational Society Project

Shyamal Sharma and Jody Hoffer Gittell

The complex nature of the crises we face

We live in a world that is highly interconnected – socially, economically, environmentally and evolutionarily. As a result, our crises are increasingly global in nature. These crises may be cumulative, as with climate change, human-on-human violence, and rising inequality. Or they may be catastrophic, as with pandemics, earthquakes, wildfires, holocausts and riots. These crises are often intertwined over time as cumulative crises give rise to intermittent catastrophic crises. And they increasingly permeate geopolitical boundaries, ultimately affecting life around the globe. These crises therefore require a global response. Yet while human beings are increasingly interdependent, we are also deeply divided by race, gender, economic inequality, nationality, religion, political orientation and more. While humans have the evolutionary capability to respond to crises through either competition or coordination, coordination is often the more practical response.

Building relational coordination within and across boundaries

Coordination is defined most simply as the management of interdependence (Malone & Crowston, 1994). To manage growing interdependence, social and organizational behavior theorists have worked to understand how people and their organizations coordinate within and across boundaries to achieve their desired outcomes (Weick & Roberts, 1993; Gittell, 2011, 2003; Faraj & Xiao, 2006; Okhuysen & Bechky, 2009; Stephens, 2021). Mary Parker Follett (1949) was the first to offer an explicitly relational approach to coordination:

> It is impossible ... to work most effectively at coordination until you have made up your mind where you stand philosophically in regard to the relation of parts to wholes. We have spoken of the

DOI: 10.4324/9781003109372-11

relation of departments – sales and production, advertising, and financial – to each other, but the most profound truth that philosophy has ever given us concerns not only the relation of parts, but the relation of parts to the whole, not to a stationary whole, but to a whole a-making.

Relational coordination theory was built on this foundation. Relationships of shared goals, shared knowledge, and mutual respect help to support frequent, timely, accurate, problem-solving communication among key stakeholders by helping them to see the whole – while relationships of fragmented goals, exclusive knowledge and disrespect give rise to infrequent, delayed, inaccurate and blaming communication among the parties involved. Both of these dynamics form mutually reinforcing cycles. Positive cycles of relational coordination help stakeholders to effectively manage their interdependence, and to find integrative solutions that enable them to achieve desired outcomes. Negative cycles enable some stakeholders to dominate others, resulting in win/lose solutions that ultimately have negative consequences even for the winners, given their interdependence with the losers (Figure 9.1).

How can change agents build relational coordination among key stakeholders to enable them to find integrative solutions that meet their needs in a sustainable way? There are three types of interventions to consider – relational, work process, and structural interventions – in the Relational Model of Organizational Change (Gittell, 2016). Together these interventions work to create and sustain positive dynamics of relational coordination, driving desired outcomes such as quality, safety, well-being, efficiency and the ability to innovate and learn (Figure 9.2).

Relational interventions aim to build shared goals, shared knowledge and mutual respect, based on principles of social psychology (Edmondson, 2004; Schein & Schein, 2021; Stephens, 2021). These interventions include humble inquiry, psychological safety, relational mapping, sharing RC survey findings with participants, role plays, conversations of interdependence and more. For relational mapping, facilitators invite participants to identify a work process that needs better coordination and is critical to their organization's success. As participants identify each role involved in that work process, they often discover more interdependent roles than they were previously aware of. They're invited to reflect together on the strength of relational ties between each set of roles, using green lines to indicate high, blue to indicate moderate, and red to indicate low levels of relational coordination. Once the network is complete, they reflect on the root causes behind

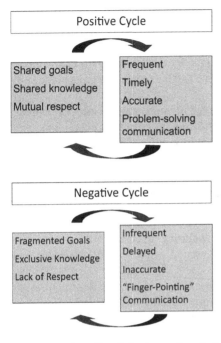

Figure 9.1 Mutually reinforcing cycles of relational coordination for better or worse

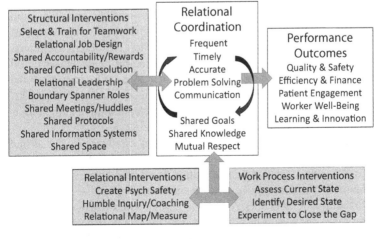

Figure 9.2 The Relational Model of Organizational Change

the observed patterns, how desired outcomes might be impacted, and where the biggest opportunities for change might be (Gittell, 2016). We have observed this mapping intervention in many countries and sectors around the world, including community-based chronic care in southwest Scotland, elder care in Tokyo, troubled youth in Denmark, behavioral health in San Francisco and the repair of oil rigs in the Gulf of Mexico.

Work process interventions are rooted in improvement science (Deming, 1986) and occur at three stages of the improvement cycle. *Assessing the current state* can be facilitated by process or value stream mapping, as well as outcome measurement by key stakeholders. *Identifying the desired state* can be facilitated by bringing stakeholders together to hear each other's needs and identify a shared vision. For *experimentation to close the gap between the current and desired state*, stakeholders identify possible solutions and experiment with new ways of working together. Through this inclusive process, work process interventions can further strengthen shared goals, shared knowledge and mutual respect (Gittell, 2016).

Structural interventions redesign existing bureaucratic structures or create new structures to support shared goals, shared knowledge and mutual respect based on principles of organization design (Argote, 1982; Galbraith, 1974). Some structural interventions, such as shared meetings, shared protocols and boundary spanners, can be introduced with the support of frontline leaders. Others, such as hiring and training for teamwork, shared conflict resolution practices and shared information systems, can be introduced by mid-level managers. Still others, such as shared accountability and shared rewards, may require top leadership support or even support from external stakeholders such as investors, customers, suppliers, regulators or policymakers. Shared accountability structures could involve leaders holding each role accountable for its impact on the organization's success, or policies holding organizations accountable for their impact on outcomes such as population health or environmental impact.

Testing the model of change. Since its initial discovery in the airline industry (Gittell, 2003) and its subsequent take-off in healthcare (Gittell, 2009), relational coordination has been studied widely in the commercial, education, healthcare and human service sectors, and in 36 countries (Table 9.1). A systematic review has discovered 81% of empirical findings to be consistent with the theory (Bolton, Logan, & Gittell, 2021). The most reliable findings thus far are about the impact of shared accountability, shared rewards and shared meetings on

Table 9.1 Industry and country contexts for studies of relational coordination

Industry contexts (n = 73)		Country contexts (n = 36)
Commercial sector	**Education sector**	**North America**
• Accounting	• Early child education	• Canada
• Airlines	• E-learning	• United States
• Asset management	• Elementary education	• South America
• Auditing	• Higher education	• Argentina
• Banking	• Medical school	• Ecuador
• Consulting	• Nursing school	
• Construction	• Primary education	**Europe**
• Electronics	• Secondary education	
• Engineering	• Translational research	• Austria
• Finance		• Belgium
• Fishing	**Healthcare sector**	• Denmark
• Information technology		• England
• Machine suppliers	• Cardiology	• France
• Manufacturing	• Care continuum	• Germany
• Multinationals	• Chronic care	• Iceland
• Pharmacy	• Community-based care	• Ireland
• Pharmaceuticals	• Diagnostics	• Italy
• Private equity	• Elder care	• Netherlands
• Renewable energy	• Emergency care	• Norway
• Road infrastructure	• Gynecological care	• Portugal
• Software	• Hepatology	• Scotland
• Telecommunications	• Health systems	• Spain
• Venture investing	• Home care	• Sweden
	• Intensive care	• Switzerland
Human Services sector		
	Long-term care	**Africa**
• Autism care		
• Child services	• Medical care	• Egypt
• Community	• Mental health care	• Nigeria
collaboration	• Neonatal intensive care	• South Africa
• Criminal justice	• Obstetric care	
• Disability care	• Oncology	**Middle East**
• Early child intervention	• Palliative care	
• Intellectual disability	• Perioperative care	• Israel
care	• Primary care	• Lebanon
• Social movements	• Psychiatric care	• Saudi Arabia
• Sports	• Public health	
• Substance use treatment	• Rehabilitation care	
• Youth services	• Specialty care	
	• Surgical care	
	• Telehealth	
	• Transplant care	
	• Trauma care	
	• Veterinary care	

(*Continued*)

Table 9.1 (Continued)

Industry contexts (n = 73)	Country contexts (n = 36)
	Asia
	• China
	• India
	• Japan
	• Malaysia
	• Pakistan
	• Singapore
	• South Korea
	• Australia
	• New Zealand

relational coordination – and about the impact of relational coordination on well-being, learning and innovation.

Following a plethora of cross-sectional studies, longitudinal studies are now exploring how relational coordination happens. Erika Gebo and Brenda Bond (2020) studied two cities that were working with over a dozen stakeholder groups to combat youth violence, comparing them to two matched cities. The two intervention cities carried out relational and work process interventions and experienced significant improvements in relational coordination across their stakeholder networks, relative to the two matched cities. But these improvements in relational coordination were only sustained in the city that also adopted structural interventions, including a boundary spanner role to continue convening stakeholders in shared meetings over time.

In sum, relational coordination is a way of connecting across boundaries to solve challenges of interdependence. Relational coordination is elegant and powerful at the same time, in that it appeals to certain fundamental values – the development of shared goals, shared knowledge and mutual respect – that are crucial for humans to live in harmony with each other and their natural environment. Relational coordination highlights the inherently relational nature of human action and offers a robust practical approach to coordinating human actions through problem-solving in response to crises. Relational coordination is a practical and flexible theory for analyzing the current state and for creating positive change. It has been supported since 2011 by a global community of scholars and practitioners called the Relational Coordination Collaborative. However, it cannot take on the larger challenge of societal change by itself. To address the interdependencies that humans are experiencing today and the grand challenges that result from these interdependencies, we need to go further.

Building a relational society

Relational society is *a state of generalized reciprocity and robust social capital, created through goodwill, empathetic fellowship, and virtuous social interactions among individuals and stakeholders in a community as parts of a whole* (Sharma, 2020). Building a relational society is a monumental enterprise. However, humans are hardwired with an innate capacity for relating with their fellow human beings, for expressing empathy, for building solidarity, for being resilient in crisis. Early in their evolution, as hunter-gatherers, humans learned to value empathy and interdependence as crucial to their survival as a species, providing an impetus for creating a social order embedded in solidarity and recognition of their shared destiny (Rifkin, 2009; von Hippel, 2018). Building a relational society is therefore possible. Building a relational society is also imperative, given the diversity and complexity of grand challenges facing human society and the larger ecosystem around it. As Reverend Dr. Martin Luther King Jr. wrote in a letter from his Birmingham Alabama jail cell (1963), humans are caught in an inescapable network of mutuality, tied in a single garment of destiny. A society of many virtuous but isolated individuals is not enough to surmount the core challenges of our day.

The Relational Society Framework offers a roadmap for how to build a relational society through three interconnected levels of engagement as shown in Figure 9.3. At the micro level, human empathy is an essential underpinning for belonging and connection; at the meso level, relational coordination enables interdependent stakeholders to engage in coordinated collective action to achieve shared goals; and at the macro level, equitable economic and social policies can be designed to support these dynamics. Actions at these three levels are in a state of constant reciprocal action and adaptation, echoing the dynamic nature of multiple ecosystems in the universe. We hypothesize that building sustainable connections and iterative feedback loops at these three levels of engagement – from empathy to relational coordination to supportive policies and institutions – will enable people to work effectively together to address a wide range of crises.

Micro level of engagement. Building empathetic connections is foundational to building a relational society. Empathetic connections between individuals have been core to the evolutionary success of humans and

Figure 9.3 The Relational Society Framework at three levels of engagement

are essential to individual health and well-being. These connections are even more crucial in times of crisis, as they tend to unlock pathways to solidarity based on shared values, in turn enabling agency for all to respond to crisis and initiate coordinated collective action for a shared purpose. The power of empathetic connection was apparent in the public outrage in the United States and many countries around the world in response to George Floyd being brutalized and killed at the hands of police in Minneapolis Minnesota in Spring 2020.

Meso level of engagement. Relational coordination enables stakeholders to engage in coordinated collective action by developing shared knowledge of each other's roles and capabilities, identifying shared goals in the presence of competing goals, and developing mutual respect. These high-quality relationships in turn help stakeholders to engage in timely, accurate, problem-solving communication to address challenges that no one stakeholder – no matter how powerful – can address on their own (Caldwell, Roehrich, & George, 2017). While this process of relational coordination often starts through micro interventions such as humble inquiry to build empathetic connections among diverse individuals, structural interventions like shared accountability and shared rewards are needed to support and sustain it, as shown above, including structural interventions developed at the macro level.

Macro level of engagement. A well-functioning relational society requires supportive policies and institutions at the macro level that complement empathy-driven engagement at the micro level and coordinated collective action among stakeholders at the meso level. It is imperative that these macro policies and institutions are consistent with democratic governance principles for distributing public goods across communities and sectors. An absence of democratic governance of public goods, especially over a sustained period of time, poses a grave risk to the sustenance of an equitable societal order, pitting various stakeholder groups against each other in pursuit of a greater share of finite public goods.

Hardin (1968) called this competition over finite public goods – "a pasture open to all" – *the tragedy of the commons*; i.e., "when each [individual] is locked into a system that compels him to increase his [share] without limit in a world that is limited". Hardin noted that this tragedy of freedom [to choose] in a commons "has no technical solution; it requires a fundamental extension of morality", perhaps akin to Bentham's goal "of the greatest happiness of the greatest number (Jeremy Bentham [Schofield, 2015])". Elinor Ostrom, a political economist and Nobel Laureate, proposed a set of *design principles* for tackling Hardin's *tragedy of the commons*. Citing evidence from numerous studies in which public goods or *common pool resources* were managed successfully with neither centralized governmental control nor privatization, Ostrom argued for a third approach to resolving the problem of the commons: The design of *durable* cooperative institutions organized and governed by the resource users themselves. Ostrom proposed that such *nested enterprises* must be established within the hierarchy of larger resource systems and political jurisdictions in order to increase the probability of lasting collective action by users of shared resources (Ostrom, 1990, 2010).

While collective action by users of shared resources can resolve the problem of the commons, macro-level governmental interventions are essential to creating a viable societal order in times of major crisis. The American Rescue Plan (2021) is an apt example, aimed at repairing widespread devastation brought upon millions of individuals, families and small- to mid-size entrepreneurs by the COVID-19 pandemic, preceded by five decades of growing inequality and social breakdown. The American Rescue Plan is a systematic intervention at the macro level to rebuild the American economy more equitably from the bottom up. There are other parallels of national and international undertakings amidst monumental global crises, such as the New Deal, the Marshall Plan to help Western Europe rebuild post-WWII, the Great Society and the 2021 global COVAX initiative co-led by the World Health Organization to accelerate equitable access to COVID-19 vaccines. Equitable fiscal and social policies like these, carried out at a large scale, are imperative for breathing new life into the lives of citizens and businesses after catastrophic events and restoring public faith in governance structures at the macro level.

The Relational Society Project: Local action for global solutions

We launched the Relational Society Project in Summer 2020 to begin the process of building a more relational society based on the Relational Society Framework. This project is being piloted in nine communities in the United States, United Kingdom, Denmark, Norway, Nigeria, Pakistan and China, with a focus on meeting the health and social needs of vulnerable populations. These nine communities were chosen for their commitment to empathy-driven relational approaches to addressing the health and social needs of vulnerable populations. Why this focus? Growing evidence suggests that persistent health and socioeconomic disparities are emerging as a public health crisis around the globe (Murray, Rodriguez, & Lewis, 2020; Robertson & Chernof, 2020; Finkelstein, Zhou, Taubman, & Doyle, 2020; Francis, 2019; Solomon & Kanter, 2018), further exacerbated by the COVID-19 pandemic. Yet health and well-being are foundational for a relational society because they are vital for individual success and for creating vibrant communities and inclusive economic growth. Because much of our health is created not in doctors' offices or hospitals but in our homes and communities (Evans & Stoddart, 1990), interdependent efforts will be required from multiple stakeholders across health and community-based social sectors.

In each community, we have started by observing what local stakeholders are already doing in response to existing crises. In Cincinnati Ohio, the largest children's hospital there has developed a network of key stakeholders to create more equitable outcomes for vulnerable children and their families. In Haderslev, Denmark, the municipality is launching an initiative among key stakeholders to focus on improving care in the first 1000 days in the lives of vulnerable children. In Abuja Nigeria, non-profit groups are working with the Ministry of Health and regional stakeholders to address a long-standing crisis of poor childbirth outcomes. In North Cumbria, UK, the National Health Service is experimenting with integrated care models to improve the physical and social well-being of the local population. In Portland, Oregon, a local stakeholder network was created to partner between health providers and community organizations to provide culturally sensitive care to diverse populations. In Peshawar, Pakistan, regional leaders, healthcare providers and community organizations have partnered to respond to the pandemic in a way that is far more collaborative than with previous crises. In Oslo, Norway and Shanghai, China, health systems are partnering with stakeholders in the primary and specialty care sectors to improve population health outcomes with fewer wasted resources. And in New Orleans, Louisiana, a local health system is working with its own clinicians, patients and community stakeholders to improve health and social outcomes for vulnerable elders.

Each community is leveraging the Relational Society Framework to first understand the relational work that stakeholders are already engaged in, then strengthen and sustain it by tailoring relational coordination and other interventions to meet local needs. Through this experiment, the Relational Society Project aims to demonstrate how citizens and stakeholders at multiple levels of interdependence can leverage relational coordination to address the systemic power differentials and relational breakdowns at the root of our most daunting population health challenges, then apply this knowledge to other grand challenges humans are facing.

Conclusion

Building and sustaining a more relational society is a lofty aim. However, the lack of cohesive social action for the common good is unacceptable when the very future of our planet and the survival of our species are in peril. We expect that the Relational Society Project will generate actionable evidence for change and a model of coordinated collective action that citizens and practitioners of all stripes can implement to address grand challenges around the globe. We are hopeful that these efforts will be well under way before the next global crisis that may further divide our society, paralyze our economy and threaten our natural habitat and survival.

References

American Rescue Plan: President Biden's plan to provide direct relief to Americans, contain COVID-19, and rescue the economy (2021). Washington, DC: The White House. Retrieved from https://www.whitehouse.gov/american-rescue -plan/. Accessed on May 7, 2021.

Argote, L. (1982). Input uncertainty and organizational coordination in hospital emergency units. *Administrative Science Quarterly*, *27*(3), 420–434.

Bolton, R., Logan, C. K., & Gittell, J. H. (2021). Revisiting relational coordination: A systematic review. *Journal of Applied Behavioral Science*, *57*(3), 290–322.

Caldwell, N. D., Roehrich, J. K., & George, G. (2017). Social value creation and relational coordination in public-private collaborations. *Journal of Management Studies*, *54*(6), 906–928.

Deming, W. E. (1986). *Out of the crisis*. Cambridge, MA: The MIT Press.

Edmondson, A. C. (2004). Learning from mistakes is easier said than done. *Journal of Applied Behavioral Science*, *40*(1), 66–90.

Evans, R. G. & Stoddart, G. L. (1990). Producing health, consuming health care. *Social Science Medicine, 31*(12), 1347–1363.

Faraj, S., & Xiao, Y. (2006). Coordination in fast-response organizations. *Management Science, 52*(8), 1155–1169.

Finkelstein, A., Zhou, A., Taubman, S., & Doyle, D. (2020). Health care hotspotting: A randomized, controlled trial. *New England Journal of Medicine, 382*(2), 152–162.

Follett, M. P. (1949). *Freedom & co-ordination: Lectures in business organisation.* London: Management Publications Trust.

Francis, D. (2019). *An evolving roadmap to address social determinants of health.* New York: The Commonwealth Fund.

Galbraith, J. R. (1974). Organization design: An information processing view. *Interfaces, 4*(3), 28–36.

Gebo, E., & Bond, B. J. (2020). Improving interorganizational collaborations: An application in a violence reduction context. *The Social Science Journal,* doi: 10.1016/j.soscij.2019.09.008.

Gittell, J. H. (2003). *The Southwest airlines way: Using the power of relationships to achieve high performance.* New York: McGraw-Hill.

Gittell, J. H. (2009). *High performance healthcare: Using the power of relationships to achieve quality, efficiency and resilience.* New York: McGraw-Hill.

Gittell, J. H. (2011). New directions for relational coordination theory. In K. Cameron & G. M. Spreitzer (Eds.), *The Oxford handbook of positive organizational scholarship* (pp. 400–411). New York: Oxford University Press.

Gittell, J. H. (2016). *Transforming relationships for high performance: The power of relational coordination.* Palo Alto, CA: Stanford University Press.

Hardin, G. J. (1968). The tragedy of the commons. *Science, 162*(3859), 1243–1248.

King, M. L. (1963). Original letter. Cited in *Martin Luther King Jr.'s Letter from Birmingham Jail: Special Issue on King.* February 2018. Washington, DC: The Atlantic Monthly Group.

Malone, T. W., & Crowston, K. (1994). The interdisciplinary study of coordination. *ACM Computing Surveys (CSUR), 26*(1), 87–119.

Murray, G. F., Rodriguez, H. P., & Lewis, V. A. (2020). Upstream with a small paddle: How ACOs are working against the current to meet patients' social needs. *Health Affairs, 39*(2), 199–206.

Okhuysen, G. A., & Bechky, B. A. (2009). Coordination in organizations: An integrative perspective. *Academy of Management Annals, 3*(1), 463–502.

Ostrom, E. C. (1990). *Governing the commons: The evolution of institutions for collective action.* Cambridge, UK: Cambridge University Press.

Ostrom, E. C. (2010). Beyond markets and states: Polycentric governance of complex economic systems. *American Economic Review, 100*(3), 641–694.

Rifkin, J. (2009). RSA ANIMATE: The empathic civilisation. Retrieved from https://youtu.be/l7AWnfFRc7g

Robertson, L. & Chernof, B. A. (2020). Addressing social determinants: Scaling up partnerships with community-based organization networks. *Health Affairs Blog,* February 24, 2020.

Schein, E. H., & Schein, P. A. (2021). *Humble inquiry: The gentle art of asking instead of telling*. Oakland, CA: Berrett-Koehler Publishers.

Schofield, P. (2015). *Jeremy Bentham on Utility and Truth: History of European Ideas* (Vol. 41, No. 8, pp. 1125–1142). Oxfordshire, England: Routledge.

Sharma, S. (2020). *Building a relational society*. Report to the Topol Family Foundation. Heller School for Social Policy and Management, Brandeis University.

Solomon, L. S., & Kanter, M. H. (2018). Health care steps up to social determinants of health: Current context. *The Permanente Journal, 22,* 18–139.

Stephens, J. P. (2021). How the show goes on: Using the aesthetic experience of collective performance to adapt while coordinating. *Administrative Science Quarterly, 66*(1), 1–41.

von Hippel, W. (2018). *The social leap: The new evolutionary science of who we are, where we come from, and what makes us happy*. New York, NY: HarperCollins Publishers.

Weick, K. E., & Roberts, K. H. (1993). Collective mind in organizations: Heedful interrelating on flight decks. *Administrative Science Quarterly, 38*(3), 357–381.

10 Global warming

The threat and the hope

Edgar H. Schein and Peter A. Schein

In this brief paper we reflect on the problem of global warming and how to begin to think hopefully about it. It is easy to focus on just the challenges for our own country but rather than deal with those, we want to focus on some whole earth issues – doing something about global warming goes well beyond what our country or your country might do or *might not do* about it.

The global Covid-19 pandemic has shown that humanity is both selfish and competitive in some respects *and* wonderfully giving and collaborative in others. In coping with the virus, we have seen incredible collaboration and generous helping within hospitals, within communities and even within countries, but when it comes to political and economic self-interest, we have seen countries continue to compete destructively. In that regard, our experience over the last few years is both bad news and good news for global warming. Let us get the bad news out of the way first.

Competition will continue to override collaboration

The world is in a very dangerous situation today with global warming because it is in a current version of *the tragedy of the commons*. The resources of the globe are limited, but each country is taking what it needs for its own nationalistic purposes – and we do not as yet see any effective global mechanism for fair allocation of those limited resources.

Only when there is a clear common enemy do regional, national and even local groups respond synchronously, as we have witnessed in some responses to Covid-19. There has been some trans-national collaboration around controlling Covid and sharing solutions such as genome sequences, therapies and vaccine possibilities. It is not clear, however, how this learning in the public health arena will help deal with global warming because the disagreements around fossil fuel and carbon emissions, energy production, land regeneration, pollution of the oceans, and methods of food production tend to fall back into economic nationalistic competitive behavior.

DOI: 10.4324/9781003109372-12

Some yearn for the "old normal" to approximate as much as possible how things were. This is understandable albeit quaint and a bit ironic as the 2020 pandemic lockdowns also allowed some people in large air-polluted cities to see vibrantly lit star-filled night skies for the first time in their lives. Still, it is unlikely that we will find enough *global* consensus to collectively mandate electric vehicles, renewable methods of energy production, regenerative methods of farming, more sustainable fisheries and so on. Efforts in all of these directions are very encouraging, even though the degree to which countries first vacillate in their agreement to join such efforts, and then fail to abide by them, varies all over the map.

Can one be confident, based on our current experience of the pandemic, that the UN, the World Health Organization and various other global entities can create and enforce a fair system of how the countries of the world will change enough to preserve the atmosphere, the oceans, and the earth in a form that will permit human survival? Or will global warming trigger another kind of global health crisis with much more serious consequences because there will not be an imminent vaccine to "cool things down?"

It is quite possible that nations will continue to only take care of themselves, and, as the Covid pandemic wanes, this may mean falling back into nationalistic competitive behavior in order to recover after the long tail of economic hardship. Even further, we may even continue to engage in cold wars, 21st-century colonialism, various forms of geopolitical domination, and even more retrograde abuses such as human trafficking, ethnic cleansing, indifference to starvation, and hot regional military conflicts. Short-run thinking makes it likely that in the long run we are indeed in danger of living out the environmental tragedy of the commons. We may soon deplete the common resources that we need to survive. In that scenario, talk of saving the planet is misdirected. The planet will survive, it's just that humanity may not.

A more hopeful outlook: Collaboration will override competition

Can we see instances of global collaboration? What drives global advances in science, literature, art and music? While there may be competition to be the most innovative, we see collaboration, not competition as the key to sustained and widespread progress. The globally uneven distribution of basic resources described above derives from the degree to which we are also *tribal*, physically organized into countries that develop their own cultures and then synchronously, but perhaps unwittingly, compete with each other and overlook the greater potential of preserving the commons instead of selfishly depleting it. If nothing else, we should seek out and learn from the best examples of the human drive to collaborate what we witness in the face of disasters and have seen within our tribes as we cope with common enemies.

Coping with the global Covid pandemic has shown us that *inside our various countries and medical systems* we are able to help each other collaborate to solve our internal health problems. Inside medical systems we have seen remarkable examples of collaborative groups that ordinarily either compete or act independently of each other, actually learning to work closely together and help each other cope with the crisis.

Our challenge is how to build on this human capacity for collaboration and continue to look for global solutions at the level of a *global consciousness*, characterized primarily by more *positive, personal and collaborative relationships* among us. Our challenge is to find a way to think globally *and act globally*, to see around and beyond nationalism and parochialism as the ultimate values, and to recognize that global warming, like the pandemic, is indifferent to country boundaries and cultures. If we can learn to think this way, what Otto Scharmer (2018) calls "leading from the emerging future, and learn to replace EGO consciousness with ECO consciousness", we may begin to see solutions that integrate both the competitive needs of geopolitical actors with our more human need to collaborate for our survival on this planet.

To begin to think this way, let's consider: (1) A global concept of *emerging* culture, the concept of *Meta Culture*, and (2) A new way of thinking about human relationships that is less *transactional* and more *personal*, the concept of *Level 2 personized relationships* (Schein & Schein, 2018, 2021).

As we will describe below, transactional relationships (Level 1) permit and even reinforce seeing each other as "objects" rather than fellow human beings (Arbinger Institute, 2020). "Personizing" means that we have to become conscious of others as whole humans like ourselves; above and beyond that they are also strangers, are from other cultures, are subordinates or professional specialized helpers, live in far-off locales and may even be our perceived enemies.

The good news is that our grandchildren and their children who grow up as digital natives, and post-digital natives, with *global* social media woven into their consciousness, may already be beginning to think this way. Even in the current generation we are seeing the growth of "global cosmopolitans", young adults who avoid identifying with any one country and are willing to work wherever their interests take them (Brimm, 2010, 2018). It is to our collective benefit to watch them, learn from them and encourage them to help us.

The concept of Meta Culture

Let's talk first about this idea of a global *Meta Culture*, as seen in Figure 10.1.

Culture is best defined as the shared concepts, beliefs, values and norms that a group has learned in surviving and growing. Any group with a history has developed a culture. The practice of that culture can best be understood, *first*, in terms of those concepts, beliefs, values and norms that pertain to the group's tasks, mission and strategy, what we can think of as its *technical culture* and, *second*, in terms of the norms of how the members of the group will relate to each other in the performance of the task, its *social culture* (Schein & Schein, 2017, 2019). Every organization has a technical culture and a social culture unique to it.

And every organization exists in a larger system such as an industry or a country that has its own concepts, beliefs, values and norms, what we can think of as the *macro culture* context. Imbalance, conflict, even war, can result when national and regional interests of the macro cultures compete with each other to fulfill their economic and geopolitical ambitions. As conflicts escalate, the risk of depleting the commons in the interests of economic nationalism becomes even greater. Yet the global reality is that national and regional interests all exist now in a connected and interdependent global system that has begun to evolve some higher order shared meta-concepts, beliefs, values and normative

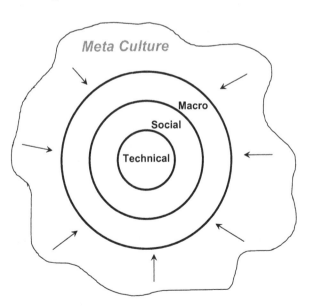

Figure 10.1 The concept of culture levels and Meta Culture

assumptions – we label this *Meta Culture* – emerging, evident yet vague, neither widely shared nor pervasive, yet.

Meta Culture is what many of us in different parts of the world can see and feel today as *globally emerging* principles, values and norms, as yet unevenly experienced and unevenly promoted and propagated. Here we think of the science fiction writer and futurist William Gibson's (2003) insight that "the future is already here – it's just not evenly distributed". Elements of Meta Culture will become sedimented gradually into the distinct cultural histories of many different kinds of groups and will increasingly influence country *macro cultures*, making it gradually more possible for countries to collaborate instead of compete.

Frederic Laloux (2014, p. 161) described new and more humanistic ways of organizing people and processes in "teal" organizations, not as isolated examples but broadly as "something in the air". In the same way that something in the air becomes common, normalized and instituted as a better way of organizing work, Meta Culture eventually becomes normalized as discernable and repeatable in the macro cultures and social cultures of national and regional organizations.

Meta Culture may be easiest to see in occupational groups such as doctors, scientists and engineers in that occupational cultures can supersede their respective national macro cultures. The details of their practices may vary by their country macro cultures and there may even be competition among subcultures on how to practice their profession, but the basic technical principles and primary professional values are global, as they are in physics, astronomy and biology. There are hopeful signs in many professions, new beliefs, values and norms around collaboration, and how we must learn to more deeply relate to each other, above and beyond our national loyalties or parochial interests, as, for example, the Russian and US astronauts have learned to relate to each other in the Space Stations.

Today's work *Zeitgeist*, when compared to last century's theories of organization and leadership, has moved us away from *linear machine* models that derived from the industrial age, toward more *organic open systems models* that reflect more realistically not only the globalization of businesses, the loosening of organizational boundaries, and the acceptance of interdependencies, but, in addition, new leadership models that put less emphasis on individual heroes and more emphasis on *leadership as a group process* in which new and better ideas come from team work and joint efforts (Schein & Schein, 2018). A Meta Culture signpost points to management and leadership increasingly becoming *team sports*.

Though Meta Culture is still vague, of variable salience, and not yet located clearly in one identifiable group, we see it clearly in some of the segments of the new generations of young people. We increasingly find spoken examples of Meta Culture in the distinct voices of young global citizens expressing a novel sense of urgency to drive change, to create a different culture in the future. Recall 17-year-old Greta Thunberg at the 2019 UN Climate Action Summit in New York saying: "We are in the beginning of a mass extinction and all you can talk about is money and fairytales of eternal economic growth … How dare you!" (Thunberg, 2019).

And there is the Prime Minister of New Zealand Jacinda Ardern who warned, that "economic growth accompanied by worsening social outcomes is not success, it is failure" (Ardern, 2019). In another context Ms. Ardern reflected on leadership: "To me, leadership is not about necessarily being the loudest in the room, but instead being the bridge, or the thing that is missing in the discussion and trying to build a consensus from there" (Ardern, 2020).

Such spoken Meta Culture examples might be seen as specific early signposts of some much broader themes:

- The Meta Culture moves away from the traditional, dogmatic and obsolete view that technology alone can solve the problem of climate change, and instead emphasizes personal responsibility, ECO consciousness and scientific realism at the center of our battle against chronic abuses of our natural resources.
- Similarly, the Meta Culture might view as retrograde the obsession with individual freedoms, accumulation and concentration of capital, and the blind rejection of any form of collectivism as having no place in a world that is now deeply afflicted with the ill effects of wealth inequality and social injustice. If we see social accountability as a central Meta Culture value, it should come as no surprise that "socialism" is no longer eschewed or feared by many younger thought-leaders. "Socialism" was a dirty word for many in the US in the 20th century. For many young global Meta Culturists, "end stage capitalism" may be far more entropic than socialism. Again, this is a Meta Culture idea that is in the air, diffuse and not yet pervasive.

Meta Culture's direct impact on national or regional macro cultures is not yet clearly discernable. We may still find plenty of young people who adhere to a 20th-century value of "American exceptionalism" and individual self-interest. If one sees this as a rearview mirror view of American ideology, consider this corollary of Gibson, that *the past remains here, and it is still unevenly distributed.*

With an embrace of the spirit of collective action there comes the realization that a variant of global democratic socialism may impact our future even in the USA, as was illustrated by the global protests that were spawned almost instantaneously by the 2020 murder of George Floyd and the subsequent reassertion that *Black Lives Matter*. While the term "democratic socialism" may need some modernization, ignoring the Meta Culture spirit behind it would be to speed past an important signpost. Instead of ignoring this signal, we might need to learn to think in terms of the new political/economic intent, not in terms of historical patterns and labels. We should not overlook the idea that the Meta Culture embraces *collaboration* and resists the abject competition that creates and perpetuates a system of owner-class control and economic injustice. Looking out a little further, a broader pattern that may emerge is a Meta Culture that deeply values *relationships, connectedness, openness* and *trust*.

From transactional to *Personized* relationships

All societies differentiate four levels of relationship as is illustrated in Table 9.1 (Schein & Schein, 2018). The lowest relationship Level "minus 1" can be described as domination and subordination of one group over another, such as in prisons or in sweatshops. We try to limit this kind of relationship in our normal business and social life, and in the Meta Culture consider sweatshops and exploitation of workers as simply unjust. While this is a form of relationship, it is negative, hence we label this Level *minus* one.

Many of our business interactions are what we are calling Level 1 *transactional* behavior based on learned social and occupational roles. We have rules of etiquette and tact that define how we deal with others with whom we transact for products and services. In the business world we have created a successful organizational model based on Level 1 relationships between superiors and subordinates. We have created a machine-like system of stable work roles that are primarily transactional and efficient based on appropriate and "comfortable" professional distance between the humans in those roles. This system has allowed us to scale up and scale down organizations as if we are flipping switches and twirling dials.

Despite the organization-as-machine's success, it is becoming antiquated, if not obsolete, as technological advances have created types of work that

Table 10.1 Four fundamental levels of relationship

Relationship level	Descriptor
Level minus one	Domination/Exploitation
Level one	Transactional (professional distance)
Level two	*Personized* (openness and trust)
Level three	Intimate (professional intimacy)

no longer benefit from static role definition. We have seen specialties come and go and we have seen that modern work requires teamwork and agility as tasks change unexpectedly.

A prime example is the enormous interdependence of the work demanded by the coronavirus pandemic. We have marveled at the ability of medical systems to adapt themselves from highly structured transactional work to the highly interdependent and flexible teamwork required to cope with overload, supply shortages and other unexpected situations. We have seen people quickly developing open and trusting relationships because getting the job done safely and effectively required it. We are calling these Level 2 *personized* relationships and have previously argued that this must happen increasingly within organizations and work groups to solve the complicated problems of today and tomorrow (Schein & Schein, 2018, 2019, 2021). We now propose that this must happen on a global scale.

We have to find a way to generalize what Douglas McGregor's (1960) Theory Y stated so plainly in *The human side of enterprise* and what is coalescing around "Theory U" (Scharmer, 2018), "Dialogic organization development" (Bushe & Marshak, 2015), "Adaptive leadership" (Heifetz, Grashow, & Linsky, 2009), "Inclusive leadership" (Ferdman, Prime, & Riggio, 2021), "Teaming" (Edmondson, 2012), "*Humanocracy*" (Hamel & Zanini, 2020), "Facilitating breakthroughs" (Kahane, 2010, 2021) and the Arbinger Institute's (2006) "*The Anatomy of Peace*". They provide a powerful metaphor – whether we approach our relationships with a "heart at war" to fight, to win, to convince, to dominate or a "heart at peace" to learn, to understand, to find common ground, to provide each other psychological safety.

We see such Level 2 *personized* relationships in companies where leaders and managers have made an effort to get to know their people and create psychological safety to reinforce openness in communication and to build trust across all the levels of the hierarchy. We have argued in our book *Humble Leadership* (2018) that such personized Level 2 relationships are the basis of what leadership has to be in the future and much of this is emerging naturally in younger workforces. We see Level 2 relationships at work as not just desirable but a presumed part of the emerging Meta Culture.

Consider these signposts: As the pandemic has created food and housing crises, we have seen widespread *unconditional help* from neighbors and strangers. Environmental organizations such as *Pole-to-Pole Conservation* (Stone, 2020) are global in their outlook, illustrated by US researchers working with the central Pacific Republic of Kiribati that is losing part of its land to rising ocean levels by helping them with their massive relocation efforts. The organization "*Heirs to the Ocean*" is organizing young "Generation Z" groups worldwide to become active in environmental education and management. We must learn to see, hear and advance organizations that reflect this important dimension of the Meta Culture.

We need a new global consciousness and new global action

What does all this mean for all of us? And what does all this mean for business and leadership educators, and our educational programs?

1) *Stay tuned to weak signals in the here and now.* The Meta Culture is expressed as much in the context of how we do things as it is in the content of what we do. In many forms the Meta Culture and its implications for the future is already beginning to flourish. Greta Thunberg's inspired environmental justice demand, the Black Lives Matter movement and many social justice movements had deep but unevenly distributed impacts on the US 2020 Presidential Election. To fail to see it and refuse to embrace it has proven to be the "wrong side of history", if not the wrong side of the future.

2) *Ask more, tell less, embrace Humble Inquiry.* If you sense there is "something in the air", it is through inquiry not brazen proclamation that you can begin to sort out what that something actually is.

3) *Take the time to understand the culture inside you, the culture you take for granted and understand automatically.* The more you understand the culture inside you, the more you will be able to listen to others, consider what is changing and the need to embrace the Meta Culture around you.

4) *Learn to think and act as globally as possible.* You may start to see how economic nationalism threatens our survival. Try resetting your focus on your global impact, and act accordingly.

5) And perhaps most important of all – *build personal open and trusting Level 2 relationships with your peers, your teams, and even with your managers and leaders.* That will propel your organizational cultures to converge with the emerging Meta Culture.

The Meta Culture is out there, unevenly distributed yet eventually central to your organizational culture. We cannot forget the stark reality that the past is sticky, resilient and unevenly distributed. Learning to discern which values and assumptions are retrograde rearview mirror forces, inappropriately resisting the emerging Meta Culture, may be as important as seeing the positive new values and beliefs. Ultimately, we somehow have to learn to absorb, and be absorbed by, this creative positive core of the next generations, even as it means abandoning antiquated nationalistic values of power, growth and profitability. As employers of younger work forces, is it not too much to ask that we learn to advocate for new global priorities of equity, sustainability and environmental responsibility?

One approach is to listen, observe, catalogue carefully what the young people around you believe and do. Like upstream flows reaching your bend in the river, it is the youthful flow of ideas, however unevenly distributed that will create cultural shifts in your future. If we are lucky it is in those flows that we will find *the balance of wisdom and innovation* required for the human species to adapt to too little water, or too much water, and too much heat!

References

Arbinger Institute. (2020). *The anatomy of peace: Resolving the heart of conflict.* Oakland, CA: Berrett/Koehler.

Ardern, J. (2019). *Global Citizen Online.* September 25, 2019.

Ardern, J. (2020). Jacinda Ardern Quotes. *Integral Leadership Review.* Retrieved from http://integralleadershipreview.com/17704-7-31-jacinda-ardern-quotes/.

Brimm, L. (2010). *Global cosmopolitans: The creative edge of difference.* London: Palgrave Macmillan.

Brimm, L. (2018). *The global cosmopolitan mindset: Lessons from the new global leaders.* London: Palgrave Macmillan.

Bushe, G. R., & Marshak, R. J. (Eds.). (2015). *Dialogic organization development: The theory and practice of transformational change.* Oakland, CA: Berrett/ Koehler.

Edmondson, A. C. (2012). *Teaming: How organizations learn, innovate, and compete in the knowledge economy.* San Francisco, CA: Jossey-Bass, Wiley.

Ferdman, B. M., Prime, J., & Riggio, R. E. (Eds.). (2021). *Inclusive leadership: Transforming diverse lives, workplaces, and societies.* New York and London: Routledge.

Gibson, W. (2003). *The Economist,* December 4, 2003.

Heifetz, R., Grashow, A., & Linsky, M. (2009). *The practice of adaptive leadership.* Boston, MA: Harvard Business Review Press.

Hamel, G. & Zanini, M. (2020). *Humanocracy: Creating organizations as amazing as the people inside them.* Boston, MA: Harvard Business Review Press.

Kahane, A. (2010). *Power and love: A theory and practice of social change.* Oakland, CA: Berrett/Koehler.

Kahane, A. (2021). *Facilitating breakthrough: How to remove obstacles, bridge differences, and move forward together.* Oakland, CA: Berrett/Koehler.

Laloux, F. (2014). *Reinventing organizations: A guide to creating organizations inspired by the next stage of human consciousness.* Brussels: Nelson Parker.

McGregor, D. M. (1960). *The human side of enterprise.* New York: McGraw Hill.

Scharmer, C. O. (2018). *The essentials of Theory U: Core principles and applications.* Oakland, CA: Berrett/Koehler.

Schein, E. H. with Schein, P. A. (2017). *Organizational culture and leadership* (5th ed.). San Francisco, CA: Wiley.

Schein, E. H., & Schein, P. A. (2018). *Humble leadership: The power of relationships, openness, and trust*. Oakland, CA: Berrett/Koehler.

Schein, E. H., & Schein, P. A. (2019). *The corporate culture survival guide* (3d ed.). San Francisco, CA: Wiley.

Schein, E. H., & Schein, P. A. (2021). *Humble inquiry: The gentle art of asking instead of telling* (Rev. ed.). Oakland, CA: Berrett/Koehler.

Stone, G. (2020). *Pole-to-pole conservation*. Nonprofit Foundation.

Thunberg, G. (2019). United Nations climate action summit. Retrieved from https://news.un.org/en/story/2019/09/1047052

Part III

Attention to development over time, and what helps accomplish it

11 Leadership in times of upheaval

The rise of the empathic leader

Amy C. Edmondson and Tomas Chamorro-Premuzic

Introduction

Leadership, the ability to enable effective group behavior, is especially important in times of crisis and upheaval (Hu, He, & Zhou, 2020). When faced with a crisis, people often feel overwhelmed by negative emotions and unable to think rationally and clearly, making them especially reliant on guidance and direction, while also in need of emotional containment (Keen , Gilkey, & Baker, n.d.). In short, they need leadership to find a viable path forward.

Upheaval brings novelty and uncertainty, reducing the viability of off-the-shelf solutions and requiring problem solving and innovation to make progress. Therefore, leadership in the face of upheaval is largely about helping individuals, groups or societies undertake a collective learning process, in which people work together to figure out what works (Edmondson, 2003a; Garavan & McCarthy, 2008). Without a playbook, leaders and followers are required to engage in systematic experimenting and learning – activities that thrive in an interpersonal context characterized by psychological safety. We propose that the emotional and intellectual challenge of this learning process calls for a leadership approach characterized by rationality, honesty and, most important, empathy (Edmondson & Chamorro-Premuzic, 2020b). Empathy, or the capacity to understand others' experiences and feelings, helps leaders engage others' willing participation in the hard, uncertain work of solution finding, while also helping them endure discomfort and sacrifice (Joireman et al., 2006).

The question of what constitutes good leadership has been asked frequently in both popular and scholarly discussions of leadership for decades (Avolio, Walumbwa, & Weber, 2009). There is a well-established stream within organizational psychology devoted to the identification of the salient attributes or qualities displayed by great leaders, dating back to the 1940s. Over the years, a sort of intellectual ping pong took shape between those

DOI: 10.4324/9781003109372-14

eager to highlight individual traits emblematic of great leaders and those focused on situational or contextual forces that shape leaders. Of course, somewhere in the middle lies a compelling resolution to the debate: the best type of leadership is that which fits the specific challenges of a given situation. And the focus of this essay is leadership in times of extreme upheaval or crisis.

Extraordinary crises leave people unmoored, anxious, unsure of what to do and of how long they can hold out, placing great emphasis on leadership for enabling an effective response. During crises, we are dependent on leadership to point the way and help us believe in the possibility of a better future. This is no easy task when the world appears to be falling apart. In more ordinary and predictable times, in contrast, top-down, detached, confident leadership approaches work. People follow because they believe leaders know more than they do, have greater experience, have better solutions, or simply because they don't think they have a choice. Without disruptions that trigger questioning of leader's legitimacy, people naturally submit to it. But crises, and the upheaval they create, are by their nature disruptive.

Research and popular recognition of the effective leadership of New Zealand Prime Minister Jacinda Ardern, largely based on her stellar performance during the 2020 pandemic, provides an illuminating case study, suggesting that effective crisis leadership respects science and facts, mobilizes collective effort, and enables coping (Wilson, 2020). Indeed, Ardern presents a striking contrast from the stereotypical leadership model of toughness and aggression displayed by other prominent heads of state, such as Donald Trump, Boris Johnson, or Jair Bolsonaro (Edmondson & Chamorro-Premuzic, 2020b). One might argue then that times of upheaval require empathic leadership, while more routine times do not. If so, this suggests that what we term *effective* leadership increasingly will be of the type that we discuss here – with empathy playing a vital role – as "predictable times" fade quietly into history.

In sum, although context matters, some attributes appear to matter in every context. For example, today's leaders (along with their followers) generally benefit from being fast learners, being calm rather than overly emotional or neurotic, and demonstrating resilience – thereby helping others do the same. It would be hard to disagree with the statement that these qualities are useful in most if not all leadership settings. But certain qualities are particularly important in crises, when leaders need a higher dose of them than during more stable times. One of these – empathy – is the focus of this essay. We argue that crises, and especially extreme crises such as a global pandemic, call for leadership that demonstrates empathy as a means of engaging others in coping, learning and problem solving.

The rise of the empathic leader in research and practice

Empathy is a quality of the human mind that transcends culture and nations. It is thought to be normally distributed within populations (Preti et al., 2010). Empathy is advantageous for leaders because influencing others is easier when you understand and can connect with them by putting yourself in their shoes. Empathizing with others is a precondition for caring about them, and leaders need empathy to attend to those who need it the most, especially in times of crisis.

In the past two decades, scholars and professionals have shown a growing interest in empathy, along with other affective, relational dimensions of leadership (Uhl-Bien & Ospina, 2012). A key construct studied in leadership research is emotional intelligence, broadly defined as the ability to identify and modulate one's own and others' emotions in order to adapt more effectively to a situation (Salovey et al., 2003). Dubbed EQ (to contrast with IQ) in the popular management literature (Goleman, 1996), emotional intelligence encompasses empathy – a capacity to detect and feel others' emotions – and its growing significance is very likely the product of our changing times. Higher levels of EQ are conducive to effective leadership because they allow leaders to take other people's perspectives, understand how people think and feel and establish genuine emotional connections with followers and subordinates. What logical or abstract reasoning problems are to IQ, emotional and social problems are to EQ, and leaders clearly need both to do their job effectively. Furthermore, as a growing percentage of logical and data-centric problems are outsourced to machines – with AI taking care of well-defined, rule-bound decisions, or at least enhancing human intelligence – the big leadership task remaining is to address the emotional problems and needs of the team, organization or community. We may not know how far AI will continue to advance and develop, but it is safe to assume that it will never be able to care about others or feel for others, and that people will surely crave human rather than machine validation.

Forces fueling recognition of the importance of leader empathy

We suggest three related factors fueling growing attention to empathy as a central ingredient of effective leadership. First, higher levels of unpredictability place a premium on the ability to build emotional connections that help people stay calm and grounded while making calm assessments and decisions. Although management scholars and practitioners have been discussing our unpredictable context for some time, often summarized by the acronym VUCA (short for volatile, uncertain, complex and ambiguous), the 2020 pandemic dramatically exacerbated the inability to predict or control results for most organizations around the world, putting a premium on a leaders' capacity to demonstrate empathy as a means of instilling trust.

The second factor is a need for teamwork to combine diverse expertise to address the complex challenges of a VUCA world more generally and in crises in particular. Expert knowledge is obviously vital to problem solving, but knowledge is distributed and must be combined to produce solutions to novel problems. Teaming across disciplines depends on empathy to help people understand and value what each other offers (Edmondson, 2012; Adamson et al., 2012). And when leaders demonstrate empathy, their teams are more likely to develop psychological safety, promoting speaking up and proactive problem solving (Edmondson, 2003a, 2003b). Empathic leadership builds psychological safety, which in turn increases a team's adaptability and performance (Edmondson, 2019).

Third, the rise of artificial intelligence as a disruptive and competing force against human intelligence has left little doubt that machines will soon outperform humans on the vast majority of *thinking* tasks, as well as in learning challenges that have an objectively defined answer. But, as previously noted, AI cannot match humans in empathy. Thus, whether afraid of or excited about AI and machine intelligence, most people believe that computers will never understand the breadth and complexity of human emotions. This makes the capacity to understand and influence emotions a more important leadership skill than ever before. Before the pandemic, most discussions of disruption emphasized technology, especially digitization, artificial intelligence and automation (Dirani et al., 2020). But Covid-19 dramatically altered that discussion. The crisis accelerated the impact of technology on work (Hu et al., 2020), not least because an unprecedented number of people suddenly relied on it while "working from home", leaving managers and leaders having to find new ways to inspire, engage, and empathize in virtual environments (McDowell, Herring, Lansing, Brower, & Meyer, 2020). Although "soft skills" such as empathy and emotional intelligence were already seen as valued leadership competencies prior to the crisis (Côté, 2014) (Harms & Crede, 2010), when leaders suddenly have to express, decode and influence others' emotions medicated by technology, the challenge intensified. Further, because AI can outperform people on objective rule-bound problem solving, the human aspects of leadership, such as empathy, acquire a more central role (Chamorro-Premuzic, Wade, & Jordan, 2018).

In sum, leadership empathy is worth renewed attention by organizational researchers and managers alike. In that spirit, we recently began a dialogue to explore the kinds of leadership that worked during the global pandemic. Our prior work on personality and leadership development (Chamorro-Premuzic) and on psychological safety and collective learning

(Edmondson) gave rise to a fruitful dialogue in which to explore the relative strength of vulnerable, empathic leadership. Reflecting on how easily incompetent men rise to leadership roles (Chamorro-Premuzic, 2019) and struck by anecdotal evidence found in current events, we have argued that national leaders who demonstrate empathy (exhibiting a noteworthy correlation with gender) have been better to manage the pandemic. Notably, comparing Covid-19 data in nations led by women and men during the 2020 pandemic reveals striking differences. As reported by Ella Lee in *USA Today*, drawing from the data base "Our World in Data", major male-led nations (the US, Brazil, Russia, Spain, United Kingdom, Italy and France) had an average of 445 deaths per million inhabitants, compared to those that were female-led (Germany, Taiwan, New Zealand, Iceland, Finland, Norway and Denmark), which had 51 deaths per million (Lee, 2020). Our argument is not, of course, that women are better leaders, but rather that personal attributes like empathy, often demonstrated by women, are instrumental in reassuring people and engaging them in the difficult work they must do to mitigate crises.

Overcoming the pull of authoritarian leadership

Empathy's value does not ensure its acceptance. Previous research has suggested that people generally gravitate towards more autocratic leaders, who display task-oriented toughness without much consideration of people's emotional needs, and exude bravado and virility during crises (Harms, Wood, Landay, Lester, & Vogelgesang Lester, 2018). Similarly, historian Ruth Ben-Ghiat (2020), using the term "strongman" leaders, explains the pull of "virility" for followers who are afraid and unsettled, whether due to a crisis or to a more gradual erosion of their standing as a result of complex social trends. When we experience fear, we may feel better if our leaders appear fearless, but this feeling may be grounded not on facts but rather on wishful thinking. Desperate for reassurance, people are vulnerable to the simplistic solutions and scapegoating offered by authoritarian leaders. Yet, the pandemic highlighted the effectiveness of considerate, trustworthy leaders, who tend to be more inclusive. The 2020 victory of the Biden–Harris US presidential campaign points to a rise in demand for empathetic leaders (Cardin, 2020) as did Ardern's global recognition for the empathic way she led an effective response to Covid-19 in New Zealand (Wilson, 2020).

In an uncertain, interdependent world, overconfident leaders who fail to listen to experts eventually fail. In contrast, leaders who focus on building others' capabilities, listening to input and embracing constructive criticism are better able to cope with novel challenges (Rashid, Edmondson & Leonard, 2013). Overconfidence is at odds with empathy, because empathy requires the ability to consider other points of view. Further, when people assert their view confidently, tying their worth or reputation to their claim, it becomes difficult for them to back down. When things go wrong, as is inevitable when data and science are ignored, "strongman" leaders, borrowing Ben-Ghiat's (2020) term, blame others and remain aloof, while empathic leaders take responsibility, earning followers' trust and support (Edmondson & Chamorro-Premuzic, 2020a). This points to a possible, and indeed pathological, gap between the type of leaders we *want* in times of upheaval and those we actually need. For example, many millions of American voters chose to follow – and vote for – a leader whose bravado and overconfidence in dismissing the Covid-19 threat imperiled countless lives. If we gravitate towards tough, macho, authoritarian leaders – and they are in fact ill-equipped to handle a crisis – then it is imperative for researchers to highlight the qualities leaders should display when times are tough – empathy being the leading one.

Psychological safety and collective action

One factor explaining why leader empathy matters is psychological safety, the belief that the context is safe for interpersonal risk taking. Extensive research examines the role of psychological safety in enabling teamwork and learning (e.g., for a review see Edmondson & Lei, 2014). Interpersonal risk is a powerful force in inhibiting the individual initiative needed to make progress in the face of uncertainty and upheaval (Edmondson, 2003a). Psychological safety is not about being nice, or providing unequivocal praise for every action, but rather about enabling the productive disagreement and free exchange of ideas that are vital to problem-solving. Empirical research shows that leadership empathy fosters psychological safety – mediated by high-quality relationships (Carmeli et al., 2009).

In a crisis, followers must be willing to take the risks of speaking up and experimenting with unproven solutions in the face of uncertainty (Rashid et al.). At the same time, they must care enough to feel responsibility for helping the group make progress – a blend of psychological safety and accountability that fuels fast learning (Edmondson, 2008).

Implications for research and practice

A core aim of social science research is to inform practice, and leadership research is no exception. The purpose of studying leadership is to select, appoint and improve leaders *in the real world*. With that in mind, we propose three implications for research and practice related to empathic leadership in times of upheaval.

First, we must rigorously examine the validity of traditional assumptions about leadership emergence and effectiveness. Scholarly and popular models of leadership effectiveness have contributed to enduring societal beliefs that emphasize strength and confidence, in relatively routine times, as well as in a crisis. Such beliefs need to be refuted with evidence. If the Covid-19 pandemic presents an unprecedented leadership challenge, this implies that prior theories of leadership effectiveness will fail to account for current events, but systematic research would lend more credibility to these claims. For us to argue that empathy plays a vital role in the effectiveness of leaders in times of upheaval, such as created by the pandemic, we must be rigorous in considering what existing theories would have predicted and what actually occurred. Further, do the highly context-specific patterns identified during the pandemic generalize to other, future circumstances? What, in other words, is context-specific and what represents a paradigm shift in our understanding of leader effectiveness?

Second, because of what is at stake for organizations and societies, researchers must rethink our strategies for ensuring that our research is used, so that relevant audiences can learn from new data-driven perspectives on how to lead. To reduce the science–practice gap, researchers must be willing to convey their findings in broader outlets. Most people are more influenced by popular writings, media characterizations and cultural stereotypes than by scholarly journals' publications of a meta-analysis. Thus, we have personally written numerous popular management articles – most recently on the need for empathic leaders – to influence practitioners. In these we draw from current events and scholarly research to develop actionable arguments. When scholars help debunk misconceptions, such as the effectiveness of the tough leader, and alert the public about the risks of appointing the wrong type of leader, people stand to gain. A silver lining of the pandemic has been its evidence that leadership matters: It matters who is in charge and what they do, particularly when results involve life and death. Social scientists can capitalize on this momentum, with its significant rise in popular interest in leadership, to inform, educate and spark debate. Social science researchers can play a role in popularizing the value of data and facts over opinions and intuition. Science offers a unique combination of data and theory – where *good* data confronts *falsifiable* theories. Still underutilized in shaping people's beliefs and views, the scientific method needs a new public relations campaign.

Third, we must recommit to providing practical steps that put science into practice. Merely understanding a phenomenon is insufficient in producing actions that obtain a better result. The ability to turn theory into a practical solution has too long been considered a second-class activity eschewed by traditional academic researchers. Although many academics cling to Kurt Lewin's famous dictum that "nothing more practical than a good theory" as evidence that their job is done, another interpretation of this statement holds academics to a far more challenging test. Lewin, we maintain, was not claiming that theory, by its very existence, is practical and should be respected as such, but rather that a *good* theory is one that can demonstrate its claim, perhaps because it makes for better practitioners, by raising the average level of performance in those tasked with putting the theory into practice. For example, many think of empathy as a personal quality that one either has or lacks, which implies that researchers face no obligation to help people develop empathy. While empathy has been shown to vary naturally across people, like emotional intelligence, empathy can be learned (Lam, Batson, & Decety, 2007). Indeed, articles on how to develop a greater appreciation for what others are experiencing and how to convey that understanding are proliferating in the popular management press, with some of these grounded in empirical research. An obvious implication of the explosion of leadership advice in online articles is a corresponding need for expert vetting. Thus, researchers have an additional role to play to help identify reliable practices that work. In short, sharing our knowledge is no longer enough. Researchers need to provide, and study the effects of, concrete suggestions to turn insights into data-driven actions. In this way, we too can adjust, tweak and improve our theories.

References

Avolio, B. J., Walumbwa, F. O., & Weber, T. J. (2009). Leadership: Current theories, research, and future directions. *Annual Review of Psychology*, *60*(1), 421–449. doi:10.1146/annurev.psych.60.110707.163621

Cardin, B. (2020). Biden-Harris Administration will restore integrity, decency and empathy to America's leadership at home and abroad. November 7th. https://www.cardin.senate.gov/newsroom/press/release/cardin-biden-harris-administration-will-restore-integrity-decency-and-empathy-to-americas-leadership-at-home-and-abroad

Chamorro-Premuzic, T., Wade, M., & Jordan, J. (2018). As AI makes more decisions, the nature of leadership will change. *Harvard Business Review*, *January*, 2–7. Retrieved from https://hbr.org/2018/01/as-ai-makes-more-decisions-the-nature-of-leadership-will-change

Côté, S. (2014). Emotional intelligence in organizations. *Annual Review of Organizational Psychology and Organizational Behavior*, *1*(1), 459–488. doi:10.1146/annurev-orgpsych-031413-091233

Dirani, K. M., Abadi, M., Alizadeh, A., Barhate, B., Garza, R. C., Gunasekara, N., Ibrahim, G., & Majzun, Z. (2020). Leadership competencies and the essential role of human resource development in times of crisis: A response to Covid-19 pandemic. *Human Resource Development International*, *23*(4), 1–15. doi:10.1080/13678868.2020.1780078

Edmondson, A. C. (2003a). Framing for learning: Lessons in successful technology implementation. *California Management Review, 45*(2), 34–54.

Edmondson, A. C. (2003b). Speaking up in the operating room: How team leaders promote learning in interdisciplinary action teams. *Journal of Management Studies, 40*(6), 1419–1452.

Edmondson, A. C. (2008). The competitive imperative of learning. *Harvard Business Review*, July/August, 60–67.

Edmondson, A. C., & Chamorro-Premuzic, T. (2020a). Tough macho leadership is over. Here's what's taking its place. *Fast Company*, October 30, 2020.

Edmondson, A. C., & Chamorro-Premuzic, T. (2020b). Today's leaders need vulnerability, not bravado. *Harvard Business Review*, October 19, 2020.

Edmondson, A. C., & Lei, Z. (2014). Psychological safety: The history, renaissance, and future of an interpersonal construct. *Annual Review of Organizational Psychology and Organizational Behavior, 1*, 23–43.

Garavan, T., & McCarthy, A. (2008). Collective Learning Processes and Human Resource Development. *Advances in Developing Human Resources, 10*, 451–471.

Harms, P. D., & Crede, M. (2010). Emotional intelligence and transformational and transactional leadership: A meta-analysis. *Journal of Leadership & Organizational Studies, 17*(1), 5–17. doi:10.1177/1548051809350894

Harms, P. D., Wood, D., Landay, K., Lester, P. B., & Vogelgesang Lester, G. (2018). Autocratic leaders and authoritarian followers revisited: A review and agenda for the future. *Leadership Quarterly, 29*(1), 105–122. doi:10.1016/j.leaqua.2017.12.007

Hu, J., He, W., & Zhou, K. (2020). The mind, the heart, and the leader in times of crisis: How and when COVID-19-triggered mortality salience relates to state anxiety, job engagement, and prosocial behavior. *Journal of Applied Psychology, 105*(11), 1218–1233. doi:10.1037/apl0000620

Keen, P. K. (Ken), Gilkey, R., & Baker, E. L. (n.d.). Crisis leadership—From the Haiti earthquake to the COVID pandemic [Article]. *Journal of Public Health Management and Practice, 26*(5), 503–505. doi:10.1097/PHH.0000000000001207

Lamm, C., Batson, C. D., & Decety, J. (2007). The neural substrate of human empathy: Effects of perspective-taking and cognitive appraisal. *Journal of Cognitive Neuroscience, 2007, 19*(1), 42–58.

McDowell, C. P., Herring, M. P., Lansing, J., Brower, C., & Meyer, J. D. (2020). Working from home and job loss due to the covid-19 pandemic are associated with greater time in sedentary behaviors. *Frontiers in Public Health, 8* (November), 1–5. doi:10.3389/fpubh.2020.597619

Wilson, S. (2020). Pandemic leadership: Lessons from New Zealand's approach to COVID-19. *Leadership, 16*(3), 279–293. doi:10.1177/1742715020929151

12 Renewing the Earth starts with renewing our capacity to work together

Peter M. Senge

Introduction: Confusing technical and cultural problems

The COVID-19 global pandemic can be seen as a kind of warm-up for what is coming, as problems like climate change, ocean acidification and species extinction unfold. It has revealed the fragility of our extraordinarily interdependent but disconnected global economy. It has drawn back the curtain on deep inequities evident in the vulnerability of different populations. It has shown how limited are our abilities to work together, even when the imperative to do so concerns relatively straightforward problems like sharing common virus testing practices and coordination of individual country and regional actions. The technical complexity of such problems masks deeper issues of distrust and lack of shared conviction that we actually *do* need to work together. In the end, perhaps the pandemic has shown us that complacency regarding the future based on our presumed technological sophistication is misplaced. Technological sophistication cannot be substituted for sophistication in the human domain, and our culture has mostly prized the former over the latter.

We are slowly waking up to the fact that problems like climate change reveal still deeper change imperatives. Paul Hawken (2017), one of the most respected writers about environmental issues, presented in his book *Drawdown* the most comprehensive overview to date of the many strategies available for addressing climate change. In his succeeding book, *Regeneration* (2021), he shifts his attention from summarizing all the things we *could do* to address the climate crisis to the underlying shift needed to accelerate actually *doing* them: "I believe the world will awaken soon to regenerative development as the only path that can restore our atmosphere, seas, land and society". Chilean biologist Humberto Maturana, architect of the famous Santiago theory of cognition, likewise points to the cultural roots of our current problems in the simple statement, "Life conserves conditions for living" (cf. Maturana, 2002). From this viewpoint, the whole

DOI: 10.4324/9781003109372-15

Industrial era stands as a sort of "anti-life" epoch, a process of harvesting inherited natural and social capital to produce financial capital. A single species, us, has benefited at the cost of enormous collateral damage to our fellow beings on this small planet. For people like Hawken and Maturana, the work at hand is not ultimately about ecology, or about business, or even about social inequalities. It is about a deep revolution of prevailing cultural norms and practices. If we are to thrive, we must rediscover what cultures that have survived for thousands of years know, that harmony – harmony with Mother Earth and with one another – sits at the core of well-being and prosperity.

This is not romantic idealism. In a global society crashing up against environmental limits, it is a survival requirement. At the present scale of the human footprint on the Earth, we are, by varying estimates, between 25% and 75% beyond what can be sustained by earth's basic life support systems. For example, the Stockholm Resilience Center estimates that four of the nine key "planetary boundaries" which assure human survival are now being exceeded, with a fifth, ocean acidification, approaching its boundary condition.[1]

But, what particularly defines the present moment is collapsing boundaries between social and ecological crises. Is COVID-19 a social or ecological crisis? The separation of "social issues" and "ecological issues" has always been a figment of our habituation to looking at an interconnected world through a predetermined lens rather than in its holistic actuality. Today, this habituation to fragmentation has itself become a primary source of suffering. The effects of increasingly stressed natural resources are inevitably distributed unevenly – the poor always suffer most. Just as devastating are the reverse effects of poverty on natural systems, like deforestation driven by impoverished farmers with few alternatives to cutting rainforests for survival. Societal crises like pandemics have their roots in ecological imbalances: As we humans encroach ever further on natural habitat, "zoonotic" transmission of viruses from a wild (non-domesticated) animal to human hosts occurs increasingly frequently. But, even deeper, they are cultural in their origins. So long as we continue to treat COVID-19 as a medical rather than cultural crisis, we will find ourselves on a treadmill of recurring pandemics.

Culture manifests through how institutions operate – from schools, businesses and families to political parties – and our current institutional ecosystem is unprepared for the systemic breakdowns we now face. Governments tend to be reactive, short term and organized around bureaucratic silos, yet the problems are long term and cross all manner of institutional and geographic boundaries. Civil society-led efforts to intervene tend to also embody fragmented mental models, driven by single-issue focused social justice and environmental NGOs, who often then find themselves competing for public attention and funding. Many businesses have attempted to become more proactive but face both public skepticism and relentless pressure for short-term results.

Put differently, we are in the early stages of an unprecedented learning challenge: how to collaborate across boundaries – institutional, sectoral and geopolitical – in ways never before realized. And, if present circumstances are any indicator, we don't have much time to learn how to do so.

Yet, we are not starting from a dead standstill. Over recent decades, there have been many steps in the right direction, some even in profoundly challenging contexts indicative of what the future will require – people and institutions working together to shift key systems like food, energy and education.[2] What are we learning from practical experiences with such "systemic collaboration" and how is this rooted in insights from social sciences applied to complex organizations over the past 50 years?

FOSTERING SYSTEMIC COLLABORATION

1. Effective collaboration for systems change is not just a matter of good intentions

Systematic collaboration is long term. It crosses diverse boundaries. And it entails challenging deeply established norms and practices. It is naive to think this is possible without developing new ways of thinking and interacting.

Effective systemic collaboration depends on individual and collective capacities that are generally underdeveloped in modern society – like the capacity to listen, to seriously consider views contrary to my own, to see how my own taken-for-granted assumptions and interpretations are part of the problem, to be aware of my own emotional triggers, to cultivate both conceptual and intuitive (or embodied) understanding of complex situations, and to embrace or "hold" uncertainty in ways that support rather than undercut commitment to action. In short, it is a lifetime of ongoing work. Lacking these capacities, we tend to trivialize truly complex issues by rigidly holding to "the right answer" and focus our energies on implementing predetermined solutions, which become increasingly unlikely to fit highly interdependent and emergent realities. Our obsession with acting quickly and believing that the key is simply more data only makes matters worse by shifting attention away from flawed mental models and low-trust relationships that prohibit collective inquiry and action.[3]

2. Three reasons systemic collaboration needs to be seen as capacity building

First, we must move beyond trivializing complex issues and yet not be paralyzed. It is a defining feature of complex systems that "cause and effect are not close in time and space" and that multiple problem symptoms emerge, each of which can invite low leverage interventions with little longer-term benefit. This easily gives rise to "better before worse" behavior where interventions focused on improving problem symptoms can make things look better for a while, while deeper sources of problems remain neglected or even get worse. Conversely, because lasting improvements may take considerable time, it is quite possible to be pursuing sound change strategies and yet see little short-term benefit. This feature can render traditional organizing strategies for dealing with complex problems counterproductive. Most advocacy movements are based on clear ideas for what needs to be done and working together to get it done. Without developing systems thinking skills, they are often doomed to the very symptomatic interventions understanding complexity warns us about.[4]

Second, to make progress, we must work together with people who are very different from us. Complex problems naturally give rise to differing points of view about what should be done. Low leverage collaboration suppresses or avoids conflicting views in favor of more homogenous groups who share common ideas. It is a simple truism that too much diversity can render any leadership group incapable of action. But, what constitutes "too much" is not fixed. A key aim of effective capacity building is to elevate a group's threshold to incorporate diverse views productively, in ways that foster deeper understanding and more effective action. This requires people becoming more aware of their own sense-making and tendencies to jump to conclusions and more capable of "sitting with" their own emotional dissonance without having their actions driven by it. When done well, people feel heard and respected *and* more safe to challenge their own views. Everyone recognizes the challenge of building trust among diverse groups, but it is a different matter to have practical strategies for doing so, such as when NGO leaders and businesses work together on complex sustainability issues (Senge, Kleiner, Roberts, Ross, & Smith, 1994; Edmondson, 1999, 2018).

Third, we are trying to get better at dealing with highly interconnected issues that no one fully understands, or ever will. Such issues are inherently confusing, not because we don't understand them well enough but because they are truly complex. The essence of reductionism lays in the intellectual conviction that there exists "the right answer" and deep-seated emotional needs for that answer. Transcending reductionism, in turn, can be thought of as a sort of individual and collective maturation process. As people start to trust one another, they feel safer to experience their own uncertainty and vulnerability. Gradually, a "capacity building orientation" can develop that displaces the need for certainty – people know they do not know, but they develop confidence in the ability to learn and get better. This is not just about how people feel – it must be reinforced by credible evidence of real improvement, discernable shifts in outcomes that are regarded as meaningful.

3. What have we learned about key domains of collaboration capacity building and how to support it over time?

Our own work (Senge, 1990, 2007; Senge, Hamilton, & Kania, 2015) has tended to focus on three critical interconnected domains of capacity building:

- Systems Awareness: a blend of conceptual understanding supported by models and ways to analyze complex issues (systems thinking) and embodied or intuitive feeling for the forces at play and how they arise and can shift (systems sensing).
- Aspiration: clarifying personal vision and nurturing shared visions.
- Reflective Conversation: fostering awareness of one's own sense-making processes and the safety and curiosity to engage in collective inquiry, that is, thinking together.

Traditional education strategies focus on developing these broad capacities independently and individually, but this fragments the core developmental processes needed for deeper learning. For example, to foster systems awareness apart from cultivating aspiration undercuts the source of motivation for the effort, to bring forth a different reality more in line with our basic values. To do so apart from reflection misses the critical role of examining how my own mental models may be non-systemic and reactionary. Just so, developmental work in each of these three domains is both deeply personal and inherently collective. Cultivating systems awareness, reflective conversation and shared vision depends on what today we call the quality of the "relational field" or space. While I may have every intention of contributing to this, real progress can only be achieved together with others.

To be meaningful and impactful, capacity building must also be integrated into actual work. While workshops and other means of focused intensive capacity building can build awareness and motivation for particular developmental paths, real capacity building only occurs over time.

Second, context matters. New capabilities must be used in settings that are meaningful for the learners in order to gauge their actual impact. We have found that coaching and meaningful peer learning groups are vital to bridge from concept to action in realistic and challenging settings. In growing a global community of master education practitioners in the new "compassionate systems" work, we have concentrated on particular geographic settings where people face similar conditions. For example, British Columbia has made unique strides in advancing social–emotional learning and tracking the well-being (beyond just their academic performance) of all children province-wide. They also face immense challenges of a highly culturally diverse population and a large number of native (first nations) children who share a history of structural racism. While all educators face common challenges of overcoming the inherited industrial age paradigm, the particularities of how this manifests vary widely, and effective peers who are already working together in the same context can be powerful learning partners.[5]

Last, no matter how useful in principle particular new capabilities might be, the outcomes achieved are almost never fully what is hoped for, and peers helping one another are essential to build persistence and perseverance. Failure is the greatest teacher. "Fail fast and fail early", may be a slogan in the software industry but it is hardly a novel insight. As Churchill reputedly said, "Success consists of going from failure to failure without loss of enthusiasm".

In sum, you need practical strategies for fostering collaboration capacity building at scales commensurate with the problems people seek to address. But there are great dangers in trying to get too large too quickly and losing the focus on deeper personal work that inevitably takes time. Two strategies stand out here from diverse projects: (1) start small: develop pilot or steering groups that learn first-hand how to build social spaces of safety and collaborative inquiry and to help others in doing likewise and (2) grow naturally by building on existing infrastructures that can extend these processes more broadly.

Start small. Practitioners often characterize this first type of work as "building containers" or "nurturing a more generative social field". Regardless of the language used, people need to build confidence that they can hold the inevitable conflict and emotion of working together on complex issues. Such images harken back to classic OD ideas like "parallel learning systems" and strategic microcosms (cf. Bushe & Shani, 1991). Regardless of the image used, this is personal work. Such "social laboratories" for ongoing experimentation and reflection cannot be created from a distance but demand personal engagement and vulnerability. As one executive leader who has been part of such a steering group in state-wide education change for several years put it, "The only thing I can control is how I show up. If I do not show up with real authenticity and openness, people who are used to working in low trust cultures will see through very quickly whatever words I use to try to get them to engage".

Grow naturally. We have seen many otherwise worthwhile systemic change projects founder on the rocks of "scaling up". Such mechanical metaphors contradict the more natural (and messy) ways that new mindsets and practices can grow and spread through infiltrating existing infrastructures that already have broad reach. In a business setting, this could mean working across business supply chains that already interconnect many suppliers and customers. In education, it could mean working with existing governmental systems of support for educator capacity building, like the work unfolding today in California's System of Support for Expanded Learning.[6]

4. None of this is easy, and it is critical to anticipate institutional counter-pressures to such collaboration capacity building and how can they be dealt with

Despite the growing recognition that we must work together in new ways to solve our most complex problems, such efforts contradict the DNA of most established institutions, based as they are on:

1. short-term focus,
2. fear of failure,
3. pressures for conformity of thinking and intolerance and even punishment for conflicting views, and
4. unfamiliarity with capacity building focused on adaptive as opposed to technical skills.

Few existing sectors of society and their organization constituents do not adhere to these cultural mandates. Most embody all four. Even tech businesses noted for their innovation by virtue of being good at the second and third conditions, usually fall prey to short-term focus and exclusive attention to technical capacity building. Some government organizations, especially those where a strong culture of mission and professional development make them good at the first and second barriers, struggle mightily with pressures for conformity and narrow technical capacity building. Universities can be good at the first three but terrible at fostering adaptive and relational competencies, dominated as they often are by narrow bodies of technical expertise and internal competition. These institutional counter-pressures need to be taken seriously – they are the reasons that systemic collaboration is so rare today despite its many espoused advocates.

Our experience is that real change starts with simply acknowledging these larger counter-forces exist and our own part in creating them. Belief that these will somehow magically be overcome by the right policies or pressures imposed from the top are naive and can keep people from finding ways to work "from the inside" to take small steps toward change. Many years ago, when a mix of business and NGO leaders were working to develop a collaboration to address the unsustainability of global food systems, it was common for the organizers to talk of being trapped in a "race to the bottom" in the industry. The CEO of Unilever, considering how obsession with short-term business goals was eroding the biological and social foundations of healthy food systems, said bluntly to colleagues, "If things do not change in this industry, in a few decades we simply won't have businesses worth being in". Rather than a grand plan or comprehensive change strategy, statements like this simply recognized the truth of the destructive forces at play in the business system they had all contributed to creating. Similarly, a state-wide education change collaboration we are now watching develop in one of the largest US school systems started with people at the state, county and local levels acknowledging that they worked in "a toxic, low trust system" that they had all contributed to creating and which rendered meaningless their aspirations to serve all children.

While there is a very long way still to go, today the Sustainable Food Lab network has played an important role in prototyping fundamental changes gradually spreading in the food industry, like tracking soil health and water use, focusing on the well-being of farming communities, and working across whole supply chains on climate adaptation. Unilever, 20 years ago a Dutch food company trapped in a history of business mediocrity and non-innovation, has become a respected global leader for industry change. After almost five years, the state-wide education initiative, a critical mass may be forming for "compassionate systems leadership for educating the whole child and shaping community well-being" as transcendent education aims.[7]

CLOSING

The word "revolution" is often used to talk evocatively about systems change, but there are different types of revolutions. Often, the word is used to point to overthrow of an established political order, though history shows that many such "revolutions" change little. But the Industrial Revolution was different. There was no one in charge. There was no grand plan. And we can be pretty sure that few in the middle of the process, especially in the early phases, used the term. Yet, gradually over a few generations, everything about society changed – institutions, worldviews, values and power structures. In effect, it was a revolution in retrospect.

Hawken claims that this is what we are living through today, a global movement of awakening to humans as part of nature versus being apart from nature. He argues that it is a movement that

> cannot be seen. It is so vast, diverse and widespread. It mutates and evolves constantly. There is no way to track it. My sense is that as certain issues become prominent, it may seem that (the movement) is shifting, but I tend to doubt that. I think what happens is that as new issues arise and become more commonly undertaken, we hear about them more. More layers are being added, like tree rings, but nothing is forsaken.[8]

Assessing the reality of something so broad and multi-dimensional as a movement toward regeneration is, of course, perilous – just as its course is impossible to foresee. If something like this is in fact unfolding, we are undoubtedly at its very outset. But, if, decades in the future it proves a valid narrative for this chaotic age of disruption, then I believe systemic collaboration will also have proven to be a key vehicle for its realization.

Notes

1 www.eea.europa.eu/soer/2020/soer-2020-visuals/status-of-the-nine-planetary -boundaries/view.
2 Examples known to the author first hand include: The Sustainable Food Lab; Climate; and The Center for Systems (www.sustainablefoodlab.org, www.climateinteractive.org and www.systemsawareness.org).
3 The importance of individual and collective reflection and greater attention to sense-making are inspired by works of people like Donald Schön, Chris Argyris, Edgar Schein and Karl Weick: https://infed.org/mobi/chris-argyris -theories-of-action-double-loop-learning-and-organizational-learning/; https://thehypertextual.com/2013/01/17/edgar-schein-organizational-culture-and-leadership/; https://onlinelibrary.wiley.com/doi/10.1111/j.1467-6486.1988 .tb00039.x.
4 Basic characteristics of complex systems are a cornerstone of diverse bodies of theory and method in systems and complexity sciences, such as Capra & Luisi, 2014; Forrester, 1994; 1995.
5 www.systemsawareness.org/who-we-are/#certified-master-practitioners.
6 www.systemsawareness.org/who-we-are/#certified-master-practitioners.
7 www.systemsawareness.org.
8 www.keapbk.com/blogs/keap/ignite-series-004-paul-hawken-the-regeneration.

References

Bushe, G. R., & Shani, A. B. (1991). *Parallel learning structures: Increasing innovation in bureaucracies*. Reading, MA: Addison-Wesley.

Capra, F., & Luisi, P. L. (2014). *The systems view of life: A unifying vision.* Cambridge, UK: Cambridge University Press.

Edmondson, A. (1999). Psychological safety and learning behavior in work teams. *Administrative Science Quarterly, 44*(2), 350–383.

Edmondson, A. C. (2018). *The fearless organization: Creating psychological safety in the workplace for learning, innovation, and growth.* Hoboken, NJ: John Wiley & Sons.

Forrester, J. W. (1994). System dynamics, systems thinking, and soft OR. *System Dynamics Review, 10*(2-3), 245–256.

Forrester, J. W. (1995). Counterintuitive behavior of social systems. Retrieved from https://ocw. MIT. edu/courses/sloan-school-of-management/15-988-system-dynamics-self-study-fall-1998-spring–1999/readings/behavior. pdf.

Hawken, P. (Ed.). (2017). *Drawdown: The most comprehensive plan ever proposed to reverse global warming.* London: Penguin.

Maturana, H. (2002). Autopoiesis, structural coupling and cognition: a history of these and other notions in the biology of cognition. *Cybernetics & Human Knowing, 9*(3–4), 5–34.

Senge, P. (1990). *The Fifth Discipline.* New York: Doubleday.

Senge, P. (2007). *The Fifth Discipline* (revised edition). New York: Doubleday.

Senge, P., Hamilton, H., & Kania, J. (2015). The dawn of system leadership. *Stanford Social Innovation Review, 13*(1), 27–33.

Senge, P. M., Kleiner, A., Roberts, C., Ross, R. B., & Smith, B. J. (1994). *The fifth discipline fieldbook: Strategies and tools for building a learning organization.* New York: Currency.

13 The social field as a teacher

Seven principles for building transformational learning infrastructures

Otto Scharmer

Ed Schein's call for social scientists to speak up and develop methods of collaboration that address the planetary emergency of our moment resonates deeply with the intention that brought me into action research and awareness-based systems change (Scharmer, 2018). When I joined the MIT Center for Organizational Learning some 25 years ago, I was attracted not only by the work of Peter Senge (1990), Ed Schein (2010) and Bill Isaacs (1999), but also by the concept of participative action research and action science (Argyris & Schön, 1989): that to know something you needed to be able to *do* it.

When we look at the primary challenges of climate destabilization, biodiversity loss, social polarization and income inequality, the main problem is not that we don't know what we should be doing. We pretty much know what the solutions would look like. According to Project Drawdown, a research project that ranked the top 100 solutions that together can reverse global warming, at least 80% of the solutions needed to reverse global warming are already accessible today (Hawken, 2017). But they are not being implemented. The real problem is the *knowing–doing gap*. It's like a decoupling of "head" and "hand" on the level of the collective. We say one thing, and we do another. That locks us into our current track of collectively creating results that almost nobody wants (destruction of our planetary ecosystems, massive unnecessary human suffering, etc.).

Which brings us back to Schein's call for social scientists to invent collaborative methodologies. At the core of implementing the UN's Sustainable Development Goals[1] and the Paris Climate Accord[2] is the need to bring together diverse groups of stakeholders in ways that shift their patterns of relationship from competition and race to the bottom to intentional collective action. Central to that shift is a mindset shift from *ego*-system to *eco*-system awareness.

How do people, organizations and systems do that? What have we as social scientists learned about doing these things at scale?

DOI: 10.4324/9781003109372-16

Systems thinking and systems sensing

My primary learning experiences can be summarized in three points. The first one echoes Kurt Lewin; the other two build on and extend that point.

- Lewin said: "You can't understand a system unless you change it".
- By extension, you can't change a system unless you transform consciousness.
- And you can't transform consciousness unless you make a system sense and see itself.

The second and third points summarize my past two-plus decades as an action researcher: You can't change a system unless you transform the mindsets of the people who are enacting the system. The third point explains how: You can't transform consciousness unless you make a system *sense and see itself*. Traditional systems thinking would have suggested that a system needs to "see" itself. But what I have learned over the years is that seeing the system is not enough. Just seeing what is broken from a detached perspective does nothing to knowledge that is transformative (Scharmer, Pomeroy & Kaufer, 2021).

The trick of any real systems change is to advance from systems thinking to *systems sensing*. Yes, I need to see what's broken with the system. But I also need to *sense and feel* the pain that others are experiencing. What I have learned is that addressing the decoupling of the head and hand on the level of the collective requires activating the knowing of the heart. *All of our senses* need to be activated. The decolonization of old-style systems thinking and the gateway to a new systems thinking starts with rehabilitating the knowing of all our senses (Goodchild, 2021). I give specific examples below. The point is that unless I can empathize with the pain and experience of the others in my system, we will be unlikely to unlock the deeper sources of collective creativity and change.

Deep learning infrastructures for transforming systems

The creation of deep learning infrastructures – infrastructures that help systems and their leaders to sense and see themselves and thus activate the capacity for transformational change – is at the core of responding to the challenges of our time.

With my colleagues at the Presencing Institute, an action research initiative at the intersection of science, consciousness and profound social change, we have conducted many experiential learning environments and workshops designed to develop deep learning infrastructures. Here are some of them:

- GAIA (Global Activation of Intention and Action): An online rapid-response initiative to the COVID pandemic launched in March 2020. This effort gave rise to a community of roughly 15,000 members who are connected and self-organizing around the world, operating in eight languages.
- u.lab 1x: This is an online MOOC offered through MITx via the edX.org platform. U.lab works like a radically decentralized classroom and has had 200K registered users since 2015. They self-organize in place-based and topic-based hubs around the world.
- u.lab 2x: An accelerator lab for teams. During Spring term 2021, 338 active teams with over 1,000 core team members engaged with many more thousands of their local stakeholders in place-based proto-typing activities.
- A three-pronged approach with more than a dozen UN organizations that focuses on helping leaders, staff and change makers to collabo-rate on accelerating the 2030 Sustainable Development Goal (SDG) agenda. The three lines of work include GAIA-style Global Dialogue events, a four-month Action Learning Lab, and SDG Leadership Labs in 14 countries.

Across these and other projects my colleagues and I have found that large-scale transformative change is possible when leaders that face disruptive challenges are supported with learning infrastructures that help them to slow down, to stop, and to attend to the deeper process of letting go (of what is no longer essential) and letting come (of what they sense is wanting to emerge). Since such periods are likely to continue, the main goal is to create deep learning infrastructures that allow people to slow down, stop, and bend their beam of observation back onto themselves. Here are seven features or components of such a learning infrastructure that we have found to be helpful.

(1) Listening: Listen to others, to yourself and to what emerges from the social field.

The primary source of learning in these experiences is not the instructor. The Reggio Emilia approach to education and learning, named after a city in Italy, is known for seeing *place* as the third teacher (with the *learner* and the *educator* being the other two). Building on that idea, I have come to see the activation of *generative social fields* as a fourth teacher. The term social field refers to the relational quality of conversing, thinking and acting together, which in turn leads to practi-cal results. Social fields are enacted from a set of mostly invisible inner and outer conditions (Scharmer & Pomeroy, 2019). *Generative* social fields are a distinct state that comes with a heightened experience of co-creativity and resonance, and a collapse of the boundary between self and other.

One participant in the GAIA journey, who himself teaches systems thinking at his university in Chile, said:

To experience real interconnectedness is not just an idea, because I teach my students about how we're one with nature, and all together kind of in theory, but I've never experienced it with other humans so openly.

We are educated to think that dreams are just dreams – the opposite of reality. In GAIA I saw in others my own dreams and it made me realize that these are collective forces shaping our common futures. In the GAIA process, I felt like a seed at the arrival of spring ... feeling the magnetic pull of collective blooming.

This gave me a great sense of trust in this inner force that wants to emerge in all of us. As a natural, organic, regenerative force that reshapes ourselves, our work and our culture.

The fourth teacher – the social field – is always there. The problem is that, more often than not, we do not pay attention to it. The main leverage point and power of the social field lies in listening. Deepening our listening by *paying attention to our attention* is an important step in shifting the social field from habitual to generative ways of operating (Scharmer, 2018).

(2) Containers: Build holding spaces for cultivating generative social fields

A lot of what you end up doing when you try to activate and cultivate generative social fields is holding the space – or, in facilitation-speak, building containers. If the quality of the results in a social system is a function of the quality of relationships, then the quality of relationships in a social field is a function of the container and the inner conditions that people bring. Building a generative container requires setting appropriate ground rules. It also involves setting shared intentions, setting the right tone, and embodying the field that you want to see through the quality of presence that you as an educator evoke.

(3) Practices: Apply awareness-based tools and practices

Approximately one-third of participants in our online awareness-based workshops report "life-changing" experiences. These often turn out to be a set of generative social practices that participants engage with in small circles. For example, the Case Clinic Circle takes participants through a structured seven-step process in which one person (the case-giver) shares a challenging situation and others (the coaches) listen, in open-minded, open-hearted and open-willed ways without offering any advice. Practices like these allow participants to learn from the social field. The generative social field is different from more traditional teachers. It lets the case-giver see her own situation through the lens of a community of coaches or listeners who are there to facilitate the best future that is trying to emerge. That quality of generative listening is the biggest gift that we as humans can give to each other.

(4) Embodied learning: Cultivate social-arts-based practice fields

We have also learned what a critical role the social arts can play in creating behavioral change. Everyone knows that change requires support infrastructures, one of which, we have learned, is social-arts-based fields of practice. All athletes and performance artists use practice fields to rehearse and try out new techniques and material. But they don't just work for performers. When transformational change is required, a social-arts-based practice field can be a safe space where groups can explore and activate new patterns of co-creative relationships. One example is Social Presencing Theater (SPT) (Hayashi, 2021). Social Presencing Theater blends constellation practices, mindfulness, resonance and social science in performance-like embodied movements. SPT allows participants to make a system sense and see itself in a remarkably short time. Its outcomes are a shared understanding of the deeper change dynamics at play, a shared language that facilitates discussion and a roadmap for focusing attention on practical next steps.

(5) Stillness and resonance: Hold intentional stillness and inquire into resonance

Another key aspect of these deep learning infrastructures is intentional stillness and resonance. "Resonance" is a term that is used in both sociology (Rosa, 2019) and practice change work. At the Presencing Institute we have developed a set of resonance practices that use intentional stillness as a gateway. For example, we often use a scribe to capture, graphically, the essence of group sessions. Like Social Presencing Theater, Generative Scribing is a social artform created by cofounders of the Presencing Institute. At the end of, say, a 90-minute session the entire group attends in stillness to the images created by the scribe. After a few minutes we ask people to share what they see, sense or feel. That process moves the visual perception from individual to shared seeing. From there we may have another moment of stillness in which people pay attention to their own deeper space of resonance and then share with each other what they sense wants to emerge.

(6) Mirroring: Bending the beam of observation back onto the observing self

The essence of systems thinking is about closing the feedback loop between awareness and action by bending the beam of observation back onto the observing self. It is that process that makes a transformational learning infrastructure transformative. It does that with tools and holding spaces or containers that create the context for using the tools. We have developed a number of these tools, all of which are available on the Presencing Institute website and in online materials. Examples include 3D mapping, 4D mapping, and in other free online live broadcast sessions that engage people in intentional stillness, journaling and resonance practices. People who see themselves through the eyes of the globally activated social field find the experience inspiring and grounding at the same time –inspiring because they can feel a field of global connection, and grounding because they are more connected to their own intention.

(7) Presencing: Building the capacity for sensing and actualizing the future as it emerges

Another practice users say has been critical for advancing their own journey of change is a presencing practice called Stepping Into the Field of the Future. It's a guided journaling and visioning process that engages participants in an inner dialogue between their current and their emerging future self. Presencing is a word that blends *sensing* an emerging future possibility and *presence*, operating from that felt connection in the now. Presencing denotes the capacity of sensing and actualizing our highest future possibility, which highlights the original meaning of the Indo-European root of the word *leadership*, which means to "go forth" or, in a secondary meaning, "to die". In our context, dying can mean letting go (of one world that we know very well) and letting come (another better world). That is precisely what leadership feels like in a moment of disruption.

Presencing has to do with cultivating our deepest leadership capacities. If we understand leadership as the capacity of a system to sense and shape its future (or to sense and step into the future), then the key to enhancing this capacity lies in progressing on that outer and inner journey. In *Theory U* I have described the inner part of this journey as the cultivation of three instruments: The Open Mind, the Open Heart, and the Open Will. The open mind can be operationalized by applying what Schein (1999) calls Access Your Ignorance. Following that trail, we can say that operationalizing the Open Heart works through Accessing Your Discomfort, and Open Will through Accessing Your Vulnerability. Leading change by allowing the world to change you.

Activating the generative capacities of a social field is an art, not a science. It's a social art that can help us to turn the massive challenges and disruptions that we face in this century into allies, into gateways to the future that wants to emerge.

Notes

1 https://sdgs.un.org/goals.
2 https://unfccc.int/process-and-meetings/the-paris-agreement/the-paris
-agreement.

References

Argyris, C., & Schon, D. (1989). Participatory action research and action science compared: A commentary. *American Behavioral Scientist*. 1989; *32*(5), 612–623.

Goodchild, M. (2021). Relational systems thinking: That's how change is going to come, from our earth mother. *Journal of Awareness-Based Systems Change, 1*(1), 75–103.

Hawken, P. (Ed.). (2017). *Drawdown: The most comprehensive plan ever proposed to reverse global warming*. New York: Penguin Books.

Hayashi, A. (2021). *Social presencing theater: The art of making a true move*. Cambridge, MA: PI Press.

Isaacs, W. (1999). *Dialogue and the art of thinking together*. New York: Currency.

Rosa, H. (2019). *Resonance: A sociology of our relationship to the world*. Hoboken, NJ: John Wiley & Sons.

Scharmer, O. (2018). *The essentials of theory U: Core principles and applications*. Oakland, CA: Berrett-Koehler Publishers.

Scharmer, O., & Pomeroy, E. (2019, October 29). Social field resonance: How to research the deep structures of the social system (blog post). Field of the Future Blog - Medium.

Scharmer, C. O., Pomeroy, E., & Kaufer, K. (2021). Awareness-based action research: Making systems sense and see themselves. In D. Burns, J. Howard, & S. Ospina (Eds.), *The SAGE Handbook of Participatory Research*. London: SAGE Publishing.

Schein, E. H. (1999). *Process consultation revisited: Building the helping relationship*. Reading, MA: Addison-Wesley.

Schein, E. (2010). *Organizational culture and leadership* (4th ed.). San Francisco, CA: Jossey-Bass.

Senge, P. M. (1990). *The fifth discipline: The art and practice of the learning organization*. New York, NY: Doubleday/Currency.

14 Being in service of collaboration

Reflection of a newcomer

Chelsea Lei

In 2007 – around the time when a few banks were starting to unravel in what would become the most severe worldwide financial crisis since the Great Depression (until the Covid-19 economic recession in 2020) – I was a junior in Social Studies at Harvard College looking for a thesis topic. After flipping through daily newspapers for a while, I hit upon the notion that crises seemed ubiquitous in the contemporary world. While banking crises dominated the headlines at the time, crises appeared pervasive in all aspects of life in every part of the world. I wondered, what is a "crisis"? Why does the world seem full of crises? And how do we deal with them?

I ended up writing my thesis about the history of the concept of "crisis" in Western culture compared to its counterpart *weiji* (危机) in Chinese culture. I found that the meanings associated with the Western and Chinese concepts of crisis converged during the 20th century, which helps account for the emergence of the popular idea that crises are occasions for "turning danger into opportunity" (Lei, 2012). The core insight of my thesis was that underlying this convergence in semantics was a deeper convergence on the level of cultural conception of history. In Western and Chinese cultures alike, the concept of crisis/*weiji* has become a signifier of modernity that encapsulates the idea that history moves as if we are thrown into an open future with virtually no guidance from God, nature or our own past experience. Uncertainty is the defining feature and perhaps inevitable consequence of this conception of history in our modern collective consciousness. As such, we are prone to recognize uncertainties in our lives and interpret our experience through the lens of "crisis".

I graduated college in 2009, feeling emotionally and spiritually adrift with the insights from my thesis. The idea that as individuals and collectives we are stuck in experiencing the world as perpetually uncertain and crisis-ridden troubled me. Even as I went about my life in a sort of normal sequence – landing a first job, going to graduate school, falling in love and getting married, entering a professional career – I kept wondering about

DOI: 10.4324/9781003109372-17

alternative possibilities for dealing with perceived crises in our lives and in our world at large. Are we really stuck with no alternatives?

The first time I experienced a definitive, felt sense of "no" to that question was in 2016 when I attended a two-day workshop in Seattle on "authentic leadership".[1] I remember walking into a modest but well-lit room with chairs arranged in a large circle, colorful hand-drawn posters hung on the wall, a sign-in desk covered with a verdant fabric and decorated by an elegant arrangement of fresh red and yellow rhododendrons in a fine ceramic bowl. In that unusual space and at the invitation of the facilitators, I conversed one-on-one and in small groups with other participants, sat still in silence, made symbolic sculptures with playdough and art and craft supplies, and journaled reflections. I did not know the terms that I would later learn about group process facilitation – what various contributors to this book have referred to as "containers", "safe spaces", "generative social fields". I just felt as if I was transported into the future where I caught a glimpse of an alternative way of being humans together. In that future, *I am* and *we are* all more curious, courageous, compassionate, creative and collaborative. In that future, *democracy* is more communal, communicative and civil. In that future, *change* may not depend on crisis.

I became fascinated by how and why a social environment could be created such that a group of people – mostly strangers from different walks of life – could experience a qualitatively different way of being oneself in being with one another in a very short time. At the time, I was starting to work for a joint initiative of the Washington State Auditor's Office, the University of Washington and the Municipal Research and Services Center to cocreate a "community of practice" (Wenger, 2009) for government practitioners interested in exploring the future of government organizations (Benson, 2015). To me and my senior partner Larisa Benson who also attended the workshop, there was something vital in the modes of interaction and qualities of connection that we experienced in that workshop. We sensed that it might lead us to figure out not only *what* the future of government could be like but also *how* we could get there.

Indeed, as we followed that sense of vitality, Larisa and I discovered a wide variety of change theories, organization development interventions and transformational learning methodologies. These included, among many others, Ed Schein's teachings on humble inquiry and process consultation, Peter Senge's writings on systems thinking, Otto Scharmer's Theory U, Etienne and Beverley Wenger-Trayner's master class on building a community of practice, and John Kotter's concept of a hybrid organization that combines hierarchy and network. In a series of experimental projects and learning programs informed by these ideas and approaches, we brought together leaders, managers and frontline staff across multiple jurisdictions to relate to one another as fellow human beings and discover how we are all working as part of a whole system to contribute to shared goals and community outcomes. Together, through many learning conversations, we developed a new perspective that the future of government could be *more joyful* (Lei & Benson, 2019), and that we could get there by mastering fact-based government grounded in social learning (Lei, Gorcester, & Benson, 2019).

An unexpected lesson that emerged from our initiative was that the most important work to positively influence the dynamics of teams, organizations and whole systems is to consistently hold ourselves open to learning what it could mean to collaborate with others as *co-creators*. Larisa and I – two individuals at the core of our collective initiative – are 20 years apart in age, different in personality, family and cultural background, and not to mention our differences in experience and professional status. Throughout our work together, we found ourselves repeatedly needing to pause and rethink our intentions, identities and our respective roles because there were no ready or right answers to clarify the ambiguities or reduce the complexities involved in a project said to be about "transforming government from the inside out". It took considerable self-reflective and relational work to simultaneously hold our fears and frailties with compassion and lean heavily into our capacities for empathy, curiosity, generosity and courage. We needed to gain awareness and intentionally shift away from deeply internalized cultural and organizational norms again and again in order to stay committed to our ultimate collaborative purpose of improving the future of government. None of the novel insights and breakthrough outcomes of our initiative would have been possible if we did not engage with the work on this deeper level (Benson & Lei, 2019).

Following the conclusion of our three-year project, I decided to enter a doctoral program in management and organization studies. Seeing the possibility of applying tangible facilitation methods to create social conditions for personal and collective transformation fueled my curiosity and determination to pursue research on the question that I had been holding since finishing college: *How do we as individuals and collectives engage with crises in ways that create better possibilities for the future?* I thought that many of the changemaking approaches that grew out of management theory and research were incredibly powerful and life-giving. At the same time, I had observed many variations of similar approaches but found few satisfying explanations of where they had come from, how they developed, and why they would work sometimes in some settings but not always. I chose an academic program where I could learn the sources and understand the original theoretical ideas underlying many of the change technologies (Holman, Devane, & Cady, 2007) that I had seen used in practice. My hope was that I could build upon those theoretical foundations and make new contributions by drawing upon my practitioner experience and doing original field research.

Looking back, I see the collective change initiative in Washington State that I participated in as a local instantiation of what Ed Schein and Peter Schein have identified here as the emerging global "Meta Culture that deeply values *relationships, connectedness, openness, and trust*". At the heart of our vision for a more joyful government of the future is the recognition that human flourishing inside government organizations matters for the flourishing of communities and whole societies that they serve. To build public trust, governments must build high-trust relationships inside. We have to work hard to espouse and embody this Meta Culture though, for it is not yet generally understood or taken-for-granted with readily available behavioral prototypes in our current mainstream cultures and institutions. A relational way of working that transcends the mere transactional while upholding the integrity of shared purpose is still too often not perceived or adequately valued as *real* work.

Nonetheless, it is important to recognize that this Meta Culture has deep roots in enduring spiritual traditions of both East and West and inspirations from indigenous cultures that have always understood the interconnectedness of life on Earth. Just think of an image of a group of people sitting face-to-face in a circle, talking, listening and relating with one another. The practice has been in use in all human societies for as long as we can remember, and it continues to find renewed expressions in today's world in all sorts of settings, from tribal governments to Quaker clearness committees, from large group interventions in organizations to Alcoholics Anonymous. There is hope that a relational approach to addressing collective problems will live on in one way or another.

The concern that I believe all contributors to this book share is how social science might help breathe more life into this Meta Culture so that it becomes more conceivable and accessible in practice in more places. In that regard, social science of the past century has given us invaluable evidence-based understandings about why it is so hard for humans to work well together. For example, humans are boundedly rational and tend to opt for satisficing over optimizing (March & Simon, 1958). Our brains are wired to differentiate ourselves based on arbitrary social categories with a bias for the groups we perceive ourselves as belonging and against those we are not (Tajfel & Turner, 1979). We are capable of imputing different meanings and interpretations of our experience of reality (Berger & Luckmann, 1967), so when it comes to organizing it takes ongoing work of communication and coordination to enact on shared concerns and make sense of how to move on (Weick, 1979).

As a doctoral student, I see that many social scientists are seeking to increase our understandings about what could make it easier for humans to work well together, given all that we know about the odds against it. Indeed, a growing body of scholarship is devoting considerable research attention to conditions and mechanisms conducive to positive social outcomes such as personal well-being, high quality relationships and organizational health (e.g. Cameron & Spreitzer, 2011). It is exciting to see academic efforts that acknowledge and illuminate the concerns and aspirations of numerous practitioners like my colleagues in American local governments who are seeking to improve organizations and communities in more positive, generative, and equitable ways.

Based on my practitioner experience, I believe that as social science continues to advance knowledge to help foster a more relational society, it is essential that social scientists take time and care to collaborate with and learn from practitioners experienced in facilitating cross-boundary collaborations for solving complex problems or as Yabome Gilpin-Jackson refers to it as the change agents and leaders who "walk and work the edge" to bridge systemic divides. These could include practitioners in established fields like public policy, conflict mediation, community organizing and continuous process improvement, as well as those in new and emerging fields such as systems integration and user-centered design. Practitioners of these fields often intervene directly in situations where consequential decisions are made and actions are taken (or fail to be) in response to crises. Working with and learning from them could allow social scientists to gain valuable insights about how and why systemic collaboration works (or not) and what could make it easier or more likely.

Graphic facilitation is one such field that I have been learning from since the time I started organizing learning networks for local governments and through the present as I study to become a social field researcher. As a professional practice, graphic facilitation involves having a practitioner playing a role dedicated to listening to people talk in a meeting and using a combination of texts and graphics to represent key information on a large surface visible to all. I offer this practice as an example here because I believe some insights from graphic facilitators may be usefully provocative for thinking about the impact of social science in a world confronting truly grave crises.

Graphic facilitators usually enter meetings in organizations or conferences standing next to a large blank wall scroll, not knowing what is to come. In the course of an unfolding conversation, they focus intently on listening to what meeting participants are saying, intuitively sensing the unspoken emotional dynamics among them, and drawing and writing on the wall scroll a useful visual representation that accounts for the group's work together. Like every professional practice, there is a gradient of sophistication and mastery to graphic facilitation. Some of the most seasoned graphic facilitators I've observed and interviewed have an uncanny ability to synthesize conversations and group interactions in visual forms that not only mirror back the group's informational content but also surface deeper relationships between ideas. They make people looking at the visuals tilt their heads and say, "Hmm, interesting, I didn't see that was possible". When asked how they are able to do this, these seasoned graphic facilitators told me that it is not about the drawings at all; it is about understanding that their role is to be in service of the group and what they hope to achieve – and help them discover what it is if they are not clear.

Like graphic facilitators, social scientists often start a research project (and, perhaps, skilled consultants start a new consulting project) not knowing what we might be getting ourselves into. We show up in research or practice sites trusting that knowledge will come as we attentively observe, record and synthesize the information generated by the phenomena with which we are engaged. I'd like to think that, among our other roles, social scientists are scribes who record and give accounts to human experience in world affairs. I'd also venture to say that, like those seasoned graphic facilitators, impactful social scientists generate reflections of our collective experience in terms and frameworks that help people see possibilities beyond what they think existed. I wonder if when asked, these social scientists might agree with the graphic facilitators that being able to produce this kind of impact is not at all about the particular tools or methods used; it is about understanding that the role of social science is to be in service of world society and what we collectively hope to achieve – and help us discover what it is if we are not clear.

To the social scientists and scholar–practitioners who contributed to this book, it is clear that our world desperately needs to rise in collaboration to deal with crises on global scales. To me, a newcomer who came of age during the defining crises of our era, what feels most interesting and vital emerging from all the conversations here is a reflective image of interconnected humans who, while boundedly rational, are in fact also capable of being *unboundedly relational*. I believe it is toward understanding this latter image of human nature that holds the greatest possibilities for impactful social science of our time.

Note

1 www.authenticcop.com/about.

References

Benson, L. (2015, April 14). Government of the future: Introducing the government performance consortium. *MRSC Insight Blog*. Retrieved from https://mrsc.org /Home/Stay-Informed/MRSC-Insight/April-2015/Government-of-the-Future .aspx

Benson, L., & Lei, C. (2019, June 18). 7 Shifts to transform government from the inside out [Video]. YouTube. Retrieved from https://youtu.be/u7m6PyQ8dxU

Berger, P. L., & Luckmann, T. (1966). *The social construction of reality: A treatise in the sociology of knowledge*. New York: Anchor.

Cameron, K. S., & Spreitzer, G. M. (Eds.). (2011). *The Oxford handbook of positive organizational scholarship*. Oxford University Press.

Holman, P., Devane, T., & Cady, S. (2007). *The change handbook: Group methods for shaping the future*. Berrett-Koehler Publishers.

Lei, C. Y. (2012). Turning crisis into opportunity: An essay on the cultural preconditions of contemporary crisis mentality through a conceptual analysis of weiji. 東亞觀念史集刊, (2), 179–218.

Lei, C., & Benson, L. (2019). Why we need joy in government. *Strategies for a More Joyful Government*, 12–13. https://www.govjoy.org/resources

Lei, C., Gorcester, S., & Benson, L. (2019, August 21). Roadmap to mastering fact-based government improvement. *Harvard Kennedy School Government Innovators Network*. Retrieved from https://www.innovations.harvard.edu/blog/roadmap-mastering-fact-based-government-improvement-gpc

March, J. G., & Simon, H. A. (1958). *Organizations*. New York: Wiley.

Tajfel, H., Turner, J. C., Austin, W. G., & Worchel, S. (1979). An integrative theory of intergroup conflict. *Organizational Identity: A Reader*, *56*(65), 9780203505984-16.

Weick, K. E. (1979). *Social psychology of organizing*. New York: McGraw-Hill.

Wenger, E. (2009). Communities of practice. *Communities*, *22*(5), 57–80.

15 Appendix

Social scientists need to speak up[1]

Edgar H. Schein

The next pandemic will be global warming and the collapse of pieces of the global environment. We already see early symptoms with the heat waves, the floods, the uncontrollable wildfires, hurricanes and other weather changes. At the same time, the virus pandemic has revealed how much our environment is capable of cleaning itself if we give it a fighting chance. Can we take advantage of what we observe globally as the positive impact of our staying home for a couple of months?

The current virus pandemic will force some shift from *rampant competition* among countries, states, hospital units and systems based on economic well-being rather than global health, to inventing processes of *collaboration* that protect the common resources pertaining to world health.

Will we recognize that we need to use or invent methods of *collaboration* on a global level to deal with the global environment as a finite resource that we are currently depleting by encouraging or at least sanctioning *rampant competition* among countries industries, and political parties?

Social scientists have found many examples of how *collaboration* is necessary to avoid the tragedy of the commons, the unwitting depletion of limited resources. Can we now put forth what we know and what we believe in to escalate *collaboration* as a central value in ameliorating the inevitable next global pandemic around global warming?

Can we show that with complex, messy, systemic, interconnected problems, *collaboration* is not only necessary but actually produces new and better innovative adaptations? In our teaching and workshops we constantly advocate teamwork, the power of group processes, and the need for distributed humble leadership. Is it time to escalate what we believe in to the political and national level?

Can we imagine at the next year's Davos conference we get the heads of Royal Dutch Shell, British Petroleum, Exxon and their counterparts from Russia, China, India, etc., into a room together and invite them to sit in a circle, begin a real dialogue, share their stories and undergo some of the

DOI: 10.4324/9781003109372-18

group exercises we have developed to illustrate *the power of collaboration and the negative impacts of competition?*

We don't have that kind of access, and maybe even our best skills in group facilitation would not dent such a group very much to think out-of-the-box and invent collectively other ways of dealing with their shareholders, employees and communities to remain economically viable.

But as social scientists we have been educated to think out-of-the-box so let's not abdicate our responsibilities and fail to use some of the skills that we do have, and take advantage, at least to speak up. The coronavirus has provided us an incredible opportunity.

If we don't speak up now, it might be too late when the global warming virus becomes the next global pandemic.

Note

1 Originally sent by email from Edgar Schein to Jean Bartunek on April 13, 2020, accompanied by the note "Hi Jean – Would you take a look at this rant and tell me whether it makes any sense and whether something like this needs to be distributed to some of [the Academy of Management] divisions or even more broadly?"

Index

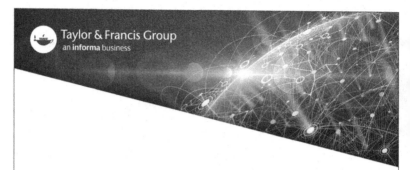

Printed in the United States
by Baker & Taylor Publisher Services